W0228470

LEGENDARY ESCAPES

SOLEDAD ROMERO MARIÑO
& JULIO ANTONIO BLASCO

LITTLE GESTALTEN

CREDITS

Legendary Escapes

Illustrated by Julio Antonio Blasco
written by Soledad Romero Mariño

Translation from Spanish by
Emily Plank
Edited by Marilyn Knowlton
Typesetting by Mike Goulding

Printed by
Grafisches Centrum Cuno
GmbH & Co. KG, Calbe (Saale)
Made in Germany

Published by Little Gestalten,
Berlin 2022
ISBN 978-3-96704-730-1

German edition is available
under ISBN 978-3-96704-729-5

The Spanish original edition
Grandes Fugas de la Historia
was published by Zahorí Books
© Zahorí Books, 2021
© Texts: Soledad Romero Mariño
© Illustrations: Julio Antonio Blasco
© for the English edition:
Little Gestalten, an imprint of
Die Gestalten Verlag
GmbH & Co. KG, Berlin 2022.

All rights reserved.
No part of this publication may be
reproduced or transmitted in any
form or by any means, electronic
or mechanical, including photocopy
or any storage and retrieval system,
without permission in writing from
the publisher.

Respect copyrights,
encourage creativity!

For more information, and
to order books, please visit
www.little.gestalten.com

Bibliographic information published
by the Deutsche Nationalbibliothek.
The Deutsche Nationalbibliothek
lists this publication in the Deutsche
Nationalbibliografie; detailed
bibliographic data are available
online at www.dnb.de

THIS BOOK WAS PRINTED ON PAPER
CERTIFIED ACCORDING TO THE
STANDARDS OF THE FSC®.

14 ESCAPE STUNT BRANDISHING A WOODEN GUN

A FAKE WOODEN PISTOL WAS ALL LEGENDARY BANK ROBBER JOHN DILLINGER NEEDED FOR THIS JAILBREAK.

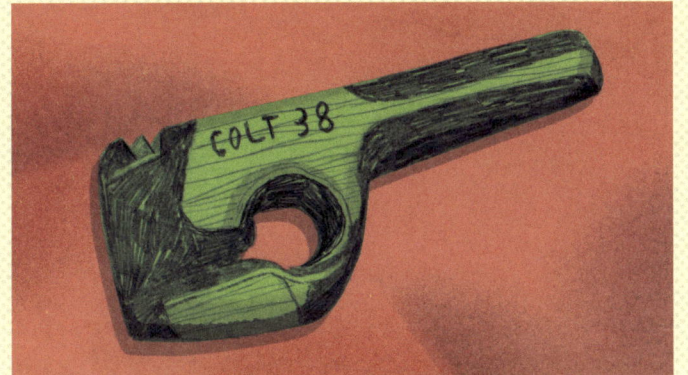

22 ESCAPIST SIMPLY VANISHES ALFRED "HOUDINI" HINDS

HE ESCAPED FROM THREE HIGH-SECURITY PRISONS IN THE SPACE OF JUST A FEW YEARS, CONSISTENTLY CLAIMING HIS INNOCENCE IN THE JEWELRY ROBBERY FOR WHICH HE WAS CONVICTED.

44 FLEEING THE GDR IN A BALLOON

TWO EAST GERMAN FAMILIES ESCAPE TO THE WEST BY AIR.

56 ESCAPE OF "EL CHAPO"

THE WORLD'S MOST FAMOUS DRUG LORD SURPRISED EVERYONE BY ESCAPING VIA HIS CELL'S SHOWER AT EL ALTIPLANO PRISON.

52 YOGI-STYLE ESCAPE

THE INCREDIBLE STORY OF THE KOREAN ROBBER WHO USED HIS SKILLS AS A YOGA MASTER TO SLIP THROUGH A FOOD SLOT IN HIS PRISON CELL DOOR.

WHEN:	WHERE:	WHO:	CONVICTION:	OUTCOME:
NOVEMBER 1, 1756	"THE LEADS" PRISON, VENICE, ITALY	GIACOMO CASANOVA	JAILED FOR BEING IN POSSESSION OF A BOOK ON WITCHCRAFT	HE SUCCESSFULLY ESCAPED AND SPENT 18 YEARS TRAVELING THROUGH EUROPE BEFORE RETURNING TO HIS NATIVE VENICE

THE DRAMATIC ESCAPE OF
GIACOMO CASANOVA

The adventurer Giacomo Casanova, the son of a merchant and an actress, spent his whole life trying to be part of the aristocracy that he was not entitled to by birth.

Thanks to his sharp mind, great knowledge, and irresistible charm, however, he managed to become one of the most fascinating characters of 18th-century high nobility.

Wherever he went, he always sparked profound curiosity and fascination. The ladies of the court surrendered to his charm, and the list of his important posts and titles was as varied as it was endless.

A master of seduction, Casanova also claimed to be a writer, as well as a merchant, philosopher, lawyer, librarian, cellist, mathematician, spy, and even a doctor. Yet behind this captivating and popular personality was a charlatan and con artist.

DOGGED BY SCANDALS AND UNDERHANDED TRICKERY, HE WAS FREQUENTLY FORCED TO CHANGE CITIES

HE ESCAPED FROM THE FORTRESS-LIKE "THE LEADS" PRISON

MADAME DE POMPADOUR WAS ONE OF CASANOVA'S MOST FAMOUS LOVERS

CHARGED BY THE INQUISITION

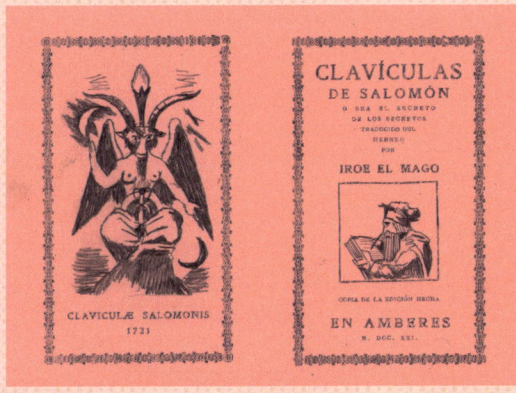

In 1755, Giacomo Casanova's meteoric rise within society was brought to a sudden halt by the Inquisition.

THE VENETIAN WAS JAILED IN "THE LEADS" PRISON, CHARGED WITH BLASPHEMY AND BEING IN POSSESSION OF A BANNED BOOK.

THE BOOK *THE LESSER KEY OF SOLOMON* CONTAINS A COLLECTION OF SPELLS DESIGNED FOR INVOKING SPIRITS, FORMULAS FOR CONTROLLING THE DEVIL, AND INSTRUCTIONS FOR ACQUIRING SUPERNATURAL POWERS AND CREATING POWERFUL TALISMANS.

ROUSSEAU, VOLTAIRE, MOZART, AND MADAME DE POMPADOUR WERE SOME OF THE FAMOUS PERSONALITIES HE WAS LINKED TO

"THE LEADS" PRISON

The so-called "The Leads" prison was situated in the basement of the Doge's Palace in Venice, at one end of the canal city's famous Bridge of Sighs.

THE PRISON OWED ITS NAME TO THE LEAD COVERING ITS ROOF, AND WHICH MADE THE CELLS INSIDE UNBEARABLY HOT OR COLD.

Jail time in this dungeon was extremely tough. The prisoners would often die of disease, hunger, and torture, but Giacomo Casanova was a survivor and managed to withstand it all.

CASANOVA'S CELL IN "THE LEADS" PRISON

THE BRIDGE OF SIGHS WAS NAMED AS SUCH BECAUSE OF THE WAY THE CONVICTS WOULD SIGH IN RESIGNATION AS THEY CROSSED IT ON THEIR WAY TO THE DUNGEON.

PLANNING THE ESCAPE

THE TUNNEL

During his imprisonment, Giacomo Casanova spent all his time and energy grinding an iron bar to make a tool, which he then used to dig a tunnel.

Over the course of several months, the Venetian dug out a corridor, but shortly before the job was done, the prison guards moved him to another cell.

It was clear that he had been watched the whole time, so Casanova was forced to devise a new plan of escape.

THE VENETIAN ADVENTURER WAS AS TENACIOUS AND METICULOUS IN PLOTTING HIS ESCAPE AS HE WAS IN RISING UP THE RANKS OF HIGH SOCIETY

THE ACCOMPLICE

To avoid being watched by the prison guards, the cunning Casanova managed to convince the monk in the cell next to his to drill a hole into the cell's ceiling.

The prison guards were suspicious only of Casanova and did not consider the monk a threat. So the monk and his cell neighbor managed to create the tunnel without attracting any attention or raising the suspicion of the prison guards.

CASANOVA AND THE MONK HID THEIR MESSAGES IN THE BOOKS THEY EXCHANGED

THE FAÇADE OF "THE LEADS" PRISON, FROM WHICH CASANOVA LOWERED HIMSELF.

THE ESCAPE IN STEPS

1. LEAVING THE CELL

On the eve of All Saints' Day of the year 1756, Giacomo Casanova and the monk slipped out of their respective cells through the holes they had drilled into the ceiling.

From the roof they lowered themselves through a window into another part of the building before leaving the palace via the exit.

CASANOVA WAS THE FIRST PERSON IN THREE CENTURIES TO ESCAPE THE PRISON

2. ESCAPE VIA GONDOLA

After fleeing the palace, Casanova and the monk went to the canal where Casanova took a gondola.

The two escapees navigated Venice's canals in the dark, leaving the fearsome prison behind and making their way to the nearby district of Mestre.

AFTER A YEAR IN JAIL, CASANOVA MANAGED TO ESCAPE ON HIS SECOND ATTEMPT

AFTER THE ESCAPE

Casanova's spectacular escape only further fueled the legend surrounding the tireless adventurer and beguiling rogue.

Following his bold escape, the Venetian continued his travels around Europe. He kept away from his hometown for nearly two decades, duping and seducing members of the nobility and royalty in the courts of the Old Continent.

THE FILM

In 2005, the American blockbuster *Casanova* brought the incredible adventures of Giacomo Casanova to the big screen.

ANTI-SLAVERY BUGLE.

"No Union with Slaveholders."

VOL. I.   NEW-LISBON, OHIO, THURSDAY, MARCH 29, 1849   NO. 1.

AN ENSLAVED MAN ESCAPES IN A BOX

HENRY "BOX" BROWN MAILED HIMSELF TO THE NORTHERN UNITED STATES, WHERE THE ENSLAVED PEOPLE HAD BEEN LIBERATED BY LAW

AFTER A 27-HOUR JOURNEY DURING WHICH HE ALMOST DIED, HENRY BROWN WAS ABLE TO FREE HIMSELF FROM THE SHACKLES OF SLAVERY.

WHEN: MARCH 29, 1849

WHERE: A TOBACCO PLANTATION IN RICHMOND, VIRGINIA, USA

WHO: HENRY "BOX" BROWN

CONVICTION: NONE. HE WAS AN ENSLAVED MAN AND THEREFORE HAD NO FREEDOM

OUTCOME: HE MANAGED TO ESCAPE TO FREEDOM

WHO WAS HENRY BROWN?

HIS CHILDHOOD ON THE PLANTATION

Henry Brown was born in the state of Virginia, in the south-eastern United States. He was part of a family of enslaved people who worked for John Barret.

DURING HIS FIRST YEARS OF LIFE ON THE PLANTATION, HE WAS TREATED WELL

Henry enjoyed a good childhood, living contentedly with his parents, sisters, and brothers.

In 1831, when Henry was just 15 years old, his master died and Henry was sent to work for one of John Barret's sons, William Barret, on a nearby tobacco plantation.

PORTRAIT OF HENRY BROWN, THE MAN WHO FREED HIMSELF FROM SLAVERY THROUGH HIS OWN INGENUITY. BORN INTO SLAVERY ON A PLANTATION IN 1816, HE DIED A FREE CITIZEN IN 1897.

THE RICHMOND TOBACCO SLAVE

The young Henry Brown was a skilled worker and was soon recognized for his efforts. It was at this time that he met Nancy, a beautiful enslaved woman with whom he fell in love. Henry and Nancy married and had three children.

They lived together for 18 years until, one day, Nancy—who was pregnant with their fourth child—and their three children were sold to another enslaver.

AUCTION OF SLAVES

Brown had previously paid his wife's enslaver not to sell her, but in August 1848, Nancy's enslaver broke his promise and sold the woman and their children to another master in North Carolina, which bordered the state of Virginia to the south.

Nobody told Brown about this decision, and he was unable to do anything about the sale. At the time, Virginia did not have any laws protecting him from suffering the same fate.

Later, in his autobiography, Henry Brown described the situation as follows:

"I had not been many hours at my work, when I was informed that my wife and children were taken from their home, sent to the auction mart and sold, and then lay in prison ready to start away the next day for North Carolina."

BROWN SWORE HE WOULD RUN AWAY AND BE REUNITED WITH HIS FAMILY

SLAVE AUCTIONS WERE COMMON IN THE UNITED STATES IN THE MID-19TH CENTURY. THE ENSLAVED PEOPLE WERE PRESENTED TO POTENTIAL BUYERS AS IF THEY WERE GOODS RATHER THAN HUMANS.

BROWN'S INCREDIBLE BOLDNESS FOUND HIM CURLED UP IN A BOX THAT BARELY FIT HIM.

THE ABOLITIONISTS OPPOSED SLAVERY AND FOUGHT TO END THE PRACTICE

PLANNING THE ESCAPE

By this time, in some states in the Northern US, slavery was no longer permitted. And luckily for any refugees from the South, abolitionist organizations were on hand to help the escaped people.

He chose the city of Philadelphia (in Pennsylvania) as his final destination, where he would be met by the abolitionist Philadelphia Vigilance Committee.

BROWN HAD THE IDEA OF PUTTING HIMSELF IN A BOX AND MAILING HIMSELF TO A SLAVE-FREE STATE

ACCOMPLICES

To do so, Brown asked two people for help: James Smith, a free black man he had met in the church choir, and Samuel Smith, a white man who worked as a local shoemaker and who agreed to help in exchange for just a few dollars.

THE ESCAPE IN STEPS

1. THE BOX

Brown hired a carpenter to build the box. He then lined the inside with thick wool to pad it and drilled small little breathing holes into the box. Finally, he wrote clear instructions onto the box to protect himself from careless handlers who might throw the box around. The box now clearly warned any mail employees:

"THIS SIDE UP"
and
"HANDLE WITH CARE"

THE BOX, AS SHOWN IN AN ILLUSTRATION OF THE TIME.

2. THE DAY OFF

On the morning of Thursday, March 29, Brown deliberately injured himself so he wouldn't have to work on the plantation.

HE BURNED HIS HAND WITH SULFURIC ACID AND WENT INTO TOWN PRETENDING TO SEEK MEDICAL HELP

What he really did, however, was to meet up with his two accomplices.

3. THE MAIL

The determined man paid his friends the mailing costs to the north and stepped inside the box with his burned hand, a little water, and some cookies.

His buddies loaded the heavy box onto a wheelbarrow and took it to a nearby post office, where they arranged for it to be sent to Philadelphia.

THE DIE WAS CAST AND BROWN SAT CONFINED IN HIS BOX

ADAMS EXPRESS WAS THE COMPANY BROWN HAD CHOSEN TO TRANSPORT THE BOX. THE SHIPMENT COST HIM $86 (OF THE $166 HE HAD MANAGED TO SAVE THROUGHOUT HIS ENTIRE LIFE).

4. THE JOURNEY

The large package left the post office by train the same day. It subsequently also traveled by steamboat, another train, another boat, yet another train, and, finally, a truck.

Despite the cautionary notes he had written onto the box, it was repeatedly struck, dragged, thrown, bashed, and placed any old way up.

But Brown moved as little as possible and did not make any sound that would raise the suspicion of the shippers.

BROWN ENDURED AN ARDUOUS 27-HOUR JOURNEY DURING WHICH HE NEARLY DIED

THE JOURNEY UNDERTAKEN BY HENRY BROWN WHILE HE WAS HIDDEN INSIDE THE BOX.

5. DESTINATION: LIBERTY

On March 30, 1849, the box arrived at its destination. The bulky package containing Henry Brown was received by Miller McKim, William Still, and other members of the Philadelphia Vigilance Committee.

When Brown was freed, he famously said what would later be made public by one of those present. He exclaimed:

"HOW DO YOU DO, GENTLEMEN?"

He then sang a psalm from the Bible, chosen specially for the occasion. Henry Brown had done it. He was tired but alive!

THE LONG-AWAITED MOMENT WHEN HENRY BROWN WAS ABLE TO STEP OUT OF THE BOX IN PHILADELPHIA AND GREET HIS RECIPIENTS.

"UNDERGROUND RAILROAD"

The Underground Railroad organization was a network of people smugglers who helped enslaved people escape.

It operated at night, when the abolitionists would transport the slaves from "station" to "station." These "stations" were often homes or churches or any safe place where they could rest and eat before continuing their journey to freedom.

The destinations would sometimes be as far away as Canada. Often, the white activists would pretend to be the masters of the fugitives from slavery so they could avoid being captured.

Following his escape, Henry Brown became a proud symbol of this organization.

AFTER THE ESCAPE

A NEW LIFE IN EUROPE

The lucky escapee, who was 33 years old at the time, earned the nickname Henry "Box" Brown and began life as a free man.

The liberated man actively fought for the rights of enslaved people in the world. He became a great orator and was considered a beacon of courage thanks to his feat.

PUBLIC SPEAKER

Brown gave a lecture in New England on the evils of slavery. He was also involved in the publication of *Narrative of the Life of Henry "Box" Brown, Written by Himself* (1849).

In 1850, his exhibition titled "Mirror of Slavery" opened in Boston.

The same year the new Fugitive Slave Act, was passed which legally required free fugitives from slavery to be returned to their owners.

Brown was forced to flee to England. He arrived in Liverpool in October 1850, alongside James Smith, his choir buddy who had helped him escape.

Together with Smith, Brown traveled around the north of England presenting the "Mirror of Slavery" exhibition.

He spent the next 14 years giving lectures at various locations and recounting the story and details of his incredible escape in a box.

In 1865, slavery was abolished in the United States following Abraham Lincoln's victory in the Civil War, and so the interest in slavery stories waned.

The story of Henry "Box" Brown, however, continued to spark a lot of excitement because it was so dramatic. Brown spent his free life performing, telling of his escape, and putting on magic and hypnosis shows that entertained fans and alarmed critics—including the abolitionists at the time.

A NEW LAW THAT PERSECUTED FUGITIVE SLAVES FORCED HIM TO FLEE TO ENGLAND

HE STARTED A NEW FAMILY IN ENGLAND AND, 25 YEARS LATER, RETURNED TO THE US, WHERE HE CONTINUED HIS FIGHT FOR THE RIGHTS OF BLACK PEOPLE

MUSIC HALL, SHREWSBURY.

FOR FIVE DAYS ONLY!

MONDAY, TUESDAY, WEDNESDAY, FRIDAY, AND SATURDAY,
DECEMBER the 12th, 13th, 14th, 16th and 17th, 1859.

MR. HENRY BOX BROWN

THE CELEBRATED AMERICAN FUGITIVE SLAVE,

Begs most respectfully to announce to the Nobility, Gentry, and Inhabitants generally that he will VISIT THIS TOWN and EXHIBIT HIS GRAND MOVING

MIRROR of AFRICA & AMERICA!

FOLLOWED BY THE DIORAMA OF THE

HOLY LAND!

Mrs. H. BOX BROWN will appear with

THE GREAT DIORAMA OF THE INDIAN WAR.

POSTER OF THE "MIRROR OF SLAVERY EXHIBITION", IN WHICH HENRY BROWN SHOWCASED HIS CREATIVITY AND TRIED TO SUPPORT HIMSELF FINANCIALLY.

THE FILM

The movie *Box Brown* (2012, dir. Rob Underhill) recounts the incredible story of Henry Brown, who gained freedom in the most ingenious and daring of ways.

Los Angeles Examiner

CHARACTER · QUALITY · AMERICA FIRST! · ACCURACY · ENTERPRISE

AN AMERICAN PAPER FOR THE AMERICAN PEOPLE · THE GREAT NEWSPAPER OF THE GREAT SOUTHWEST

VOL. XXXI-NO. 82 · For complete Weather Reports Sea Page 7. Part II · LOS ANGELES, SATURDAY, MARCH 3, 1934 · ⊛⊛CCC · Two Sec.-Part I-FIVE CENTS

WELL-KNOWN GANGSTER JOHN DILLINGER ESCAPES FROM A HIGH-SECURITY PRISON RIDING IN THE SHERIFF'S CAR

ESCAPE STUNT
BRANDISHING A WOODEN GUN!

JOHN H. DILLINGER

CELEBRATED BANK ROBBER

Born in Indiana, USA, in 1903, the rebellious youngster grew up dirt poor, roaming the streets of Mooresville.

Although he had enlisted in the navy, military life wasn't for him. With not a cent to his name, he teamed up with a friend from his hometown to rob a grocery store, but the robbery was a flop. The police caught them, and Dillinger ended up spending eight and a half years behind bars.

Prison turned out to be his school; it was there that he learned all there was to know about robbing a bank.

When Dillinger was eventually released on probation, he immediately formed his own gang. This marked the start of his career as a bank robber—until he was arrested again one year later, prompting his iconic escape.

A HANDSOME MAN, DILLINGER WAS VERY POPULAR. DURING THOSE YEARS OF EXTREME POVERTY, HE BECAME A HERO TO MANY CITIZENS WHO WERE CRITICAL OF THE SYSTEM.

WHEN:	WHERE:	WHO:	CONVICTION:	OUTCOME:
MARCH 3, 1934	CROWN POINT JAIL, LAKE COUNTY, INDIANA, USA	JOHN HERBERT DILLINGER	DILLINGER WAS CONVICTED OF ROBBING BANKS, BUT HE WAS NEVER ACTUALLY CONVICTED OF MURDER.	HE ESCAPED, BUT FOUR MONTHS LATER, HE WAS GUNNED DOWN BY CHICAGO POLICE AS HE WAS LEAVING A MOVIE THEATER.

THE WILY DILLINGER ESCAPED FROM CROWN POINT JAIL WITHOUT ANY OUTSIDE HELP AND HEADED FOR CHICAGO AT THE WHEEL OF A FORD V8, THE POLICE CAR OF LOCAL SHERIFF LILLIAN HOLLEY. HE LEFT THE PRISON BEHIND, BOUND FOR CHICAGO.

THE STUFF OF LEGENDS

"PERFECT" ROBBERIES

As a young man, Dillinger embarked on an unstoppable criminal career that helped him become one of the most creative and glamorous gangsters in all of American criminal history.

With his gang, Dillinger robbed numerous banks around the country, having devised an effective strategy for meticulously choosing his targets.

They robbed small banks in small towns with little surveillance but good access to narrow streets, which enabled them to easily escape to a secure hiding place.

The robberies took barely five minutes. The goal was to not spill a single drop of blood; that way, they risked only shorter sentences.

With spectacular staging, the robbers entered armed with machine guns and pistols, shouting, "Everybody get on the ground."

They took hostages as a safe way of fleeing without being shot down by police.

WITHOUT A WORD

Intimidated by the gang, the customers and staff put up no resistance. In just a few minutes, the robbers managed to grab all the cash and make a speedy exit.

Without ever injuring or killing anyone, yet still securing a sizable stash, they would repeat the same strategy time after time.

THE PEOPLE RESPECTED HIM FOR STANDING UP TO A CORRUPT SYSTEM ◆

FAR FROM SPARKING FEAR OR ANGER, THE STRANGE GANG GAINED PEOPLE'S ADMIRATION, AND ITS LEADER WAS CONSIDERED A ROBIN HOOD–LIKE FIGURE

DILLINGER WASN'T YOUR AVERAGE ROBBER, AND HE BECAME KNOWN IN PARTICULAR FOR HOW WELL HE TREATED HIS HOSTAGES AND FOR THE WAY HE WOULD FLIRT WITH THE FEMALE BANK TELLERS.

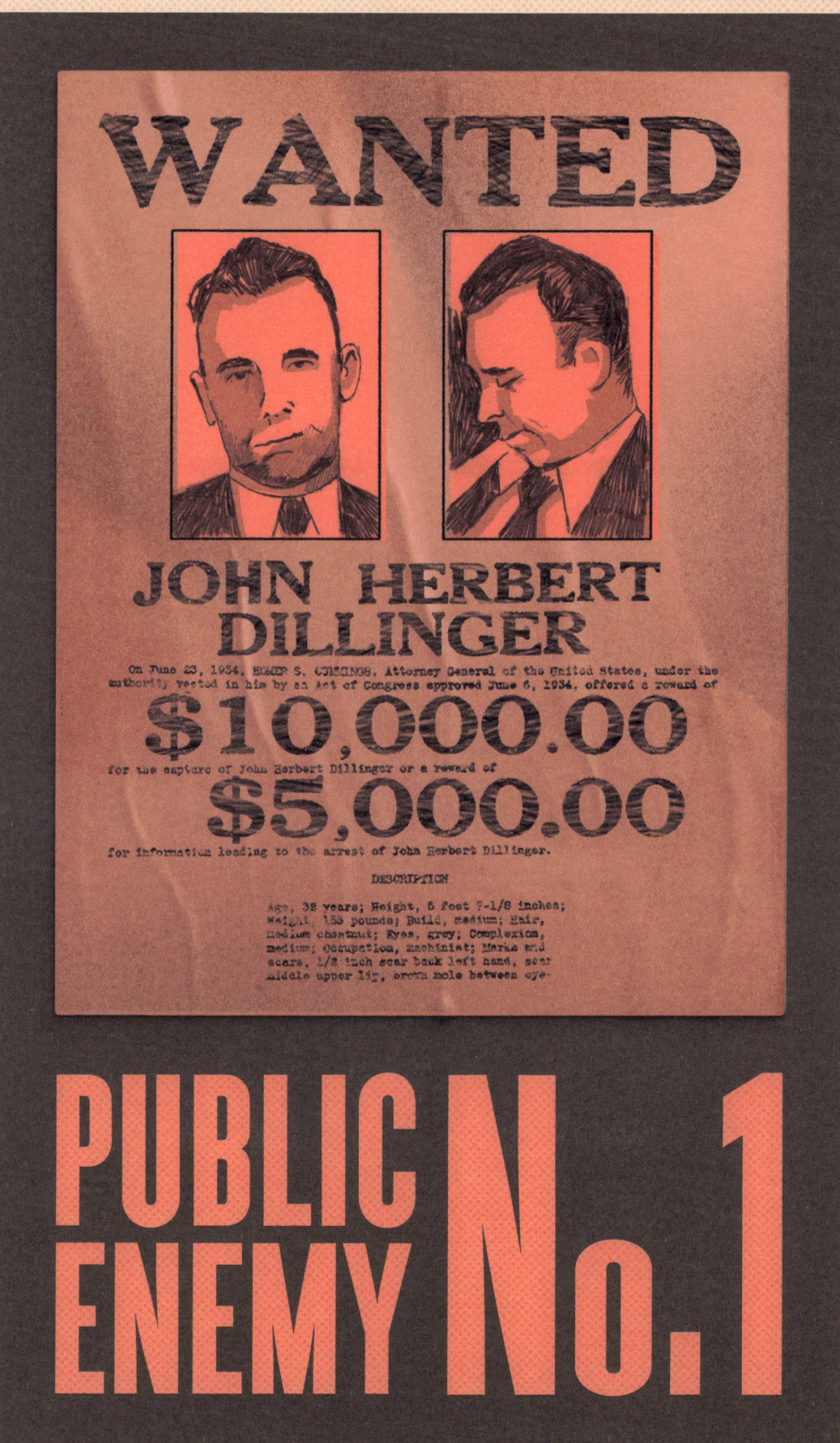

MOCKERY AND MALICE

The police were unable to beat the gang—they always arrived too late, by which time Dillinger had already fled with bags full of cash. Large rewards were offered to anyone who would turn him in, dead or alive. The "wanted" posters made him a national legend.

Meanwhile, the robbers continued to live it up, celebrating their successes by drinking bottles of champagne in luxury hotels.

IN THE YEARS 1933 AND 1934, THE GANG STOLE NEARLY $1 MILLION

BACK TO JAIL

Their run of good luck ended on January 15, 1934, while the gang was robbing a bank in Chicago. During this shootout, Dillinger killed a policeman. He was captured and sent to the high-security Crown Point Jail.

Sheriff Lillian Holley's assistants, armed with rifles, guarded the prison building, but the escape took place within the prison walls.

THE EXTREME SURVEILLANCE DIDN'T STOP DILLINGER FROM SURPRISING EVERYONE WITH HIS CRAZY ESCAPE

THE SECURITY GUARD WAS CAUGHT BY SURPRISE WHEN DILLINGER FORCED HIM TO OPEN HIS CELL BRANDISHING A WOODEN GUN.

THE ESCAPE IN STEPS
A JAILBREAK THAT FUELED THE DILLINGER LEGEND

1. A FAKE REVOLVER

During his time in jail, Dillinger came up with the ingenious idea of using an ordinary razor blade to sculpt a piece of wood into a replica revolver.

The skilled prisoner honed the piece to perfection, darkening it with the black polish he used to shine his shoes.

This was probably the main reason why the Crown Point guards did not see through the gangster's clever ruse.

DILLINGER FASHIONED THE "KEY" THAT WOULD OPEN THE PRISON DOORS FOR HIM FROM A PIECE OF WOOD

2. A NAÏVE GUARD

On March 3, 1934, the famous bank robber pointed his fake revolver at the guard. The young man believed the gun was real and opened the cell door.

THE LEGEND SURROUNDING THE GANGSTER WAS SO GREAT THAT THE GUARD DIDN'T THINK TO QUESTION THE AUTHENTICITY OF THE WEAPON

The guards Dillinger came across on his way out of jail were all stripped of their guns as soon as the bank robber managed to secure real machine guns from the police arsenal.

3. GUARDS AS PRISONERS

Flaunting a machine gun in each hand, Dillinger overtook more than a dozen policemen. Some even ended up imprisoned in the cells of the notorious Crown Point Jail.

THE PROCLAIMED "PUBLIC ENEMY NO. 1" DISPLAYED HIS GREAT CREATIVITY AND DEMONSTRATED HIS GREAT COURAGE

Finally, the coast was clear for the formidable robber, who was able to leave the prison in which he had been incarcerated less than two months before.

4. IN THE SHERIFF'S CAR

After having tricked the jail's security guards successfully, the fearsome fugitive wrapped up his escape by robbing Sheriff Lillian Holley's Ford V8 sedan and speeding off to Chicago in the police car.

STEALING THE SHERIFF'S CAR WAS DILLINGER'S ONE BIG MISTAKE, AND IT ENDED UP COSTING HIM HIS LIFE

Headlines across the US mocked the authorities for their failure to handle the situation, boosting the robber's fame even more, if that were possible.

A WOODEN GUN.
THAT WAS ALL GANGSTER JOHN DILLINGER NEEDED TO GET OUT OF JAIL AND FIND HIS WAY TO FREEDOM. THE FEAR THE ESCAPEE INSTILLED IN OTHERS DID THE REST.

5. DESTINATION: CHICAGO

The fugitive, now wanted in five states, sought refuge in Chicago with his girlfriend, Evelyn Frechette, whom he had met a few months before.

In those days, Chicago was a mafia hotspot. It was here that Dillinger managed to team up with other powerful criminals to continue his bank-robbing career.

THE FBI HOT ON HIS HEELS

AS SLIPPERY AS AN EEL, DILLINGER ALWAYS MANAGED TO FIND A WAY TO ESCAPE. FEDERAL AGENTS COULDN'T FIGURE OUT HOW TO CATCH HIM.

Without realizing it, the "Public Enemy No. 1" committed one major error during his escape—he crossed a state border in a stolen car, thereby breaking a federal law. From that moment, the FBI was able to intervene and use all means available to capture him.

From then on, ruthless federal agent Melvin Purvis from the Chicago bureau of the FBI was breathing down the famous robber's neck. He was determined not to be conned by Dillinger.

Agent Purvis spent many months putting all his energy into catching him, but the fugitive always managed to successfully evade every situation. He dodged bullets in shoot-outs with police and disappeared without a trace.

DILLINGER WAS SAID TO HAVE UNDERGONE COSMETIC SURGERY TO ALTER BOTH HIS FINGERPRINTS AND FACIAL FEATURES

As Purvis started to get desperate, he received a call that would change everything. The robber had been identified by a Romanian woman who called herself Anna Sage—even though her real name was Ana Cumpanas.

Sage had met Dillinger through his new girlfriend, Polly Hamilton. She decided to hand him to the FBI rather than be deported back to her own country by the Immigration Office. She told Purvis how to find him.

◆

DURING THE NIGHT OF JULY 22, 1934, THE LEGENDARY ROBBER'S LUCK RAN OUT AT LAST

SECURITY AGENTS, ATTEMPTING TO CATCH THE FUGITIVE DILLINGER, INSPECTED HIGHWAY VEHICLES.

ANNA SAGE CONTACTED THE FBI AFTER RECOGNIZING JOHN DILLINGER.

ANNA SAGE WAS TAGGING ALONG WITH JOHN DILLINGER, AND THE FBI AGENTS SWIFTLY LOCATED THE ESCAPEE. WHEN HE REALIZED HE WAS BEING FOLLOWED, HE TRIED TO PULL OUT HIS REVOLVER BUT WAS GUNNED DOWN.

AMBUSHED BY POLICE

THE ORANGE SKIRT

Anna Sage met up with Dillinger and his girlfriend, Polly, to watch a movie on July 22. The day before, Sage had advised Purvis that they would be heading to either the Biograph or the Marbro Theater and that she would be wearing an orange skirt for easy identification as they exited.

They chose the Biograph Theater. The screening ended after 10.30 p. m. Federal agents were tensely waiting outside for Dillinger. The gangster left the theater with Hamilton and Sage, and started walking. When he realized that he was being followed, he took out his revolver—but he never got to shoot it before being shot himself. He collapsed on the sidewalk riddled with bullets.

Fate had dealt Dillinger an ironic final blow—the robber had just stepped out after watching Manhattan Melodrama, a movie starring Clark Gable, who played a gangster sentenced to death for his crimes.

DILLINGER DIED AT THE AGE OF 31, IN A POLICE TRAP OUTSIDE THE BIOGRAPH THEATER

THE FILM

Starring Johnny Depp and directed by Michael Mann, *Public Enemies* (2009) was inspired by Dillinger's life. Two other films titled *Dillinger* had been released earlier—in 1945 (dir. Max Nosseck) and 1973 (dir. John Milius).

Daily Mirror

FRI NOV 25

2D FORWARD WITH THE PEOPLE
Nr. 16,138

ESCAPIST SIMPLY VANISHES: ALFRED "HOUDINI" HINDS

THE ROBBER ESCAPED FROM NOTTINGHAM JAIL, WHERE HE WAS SERVING TIME

HE "MAGICALLY" ESCAPED—JUST LIKE THE FAMOUS MAGICIAN HOUDINI

THE HIGH WALLS OF NOTTINGHAM PRISON, MEASURING NEARLY 20 FEET, POSED NO OBSTACLE FOR ALFRED HINDS IN HIS DARING ESCAPE.

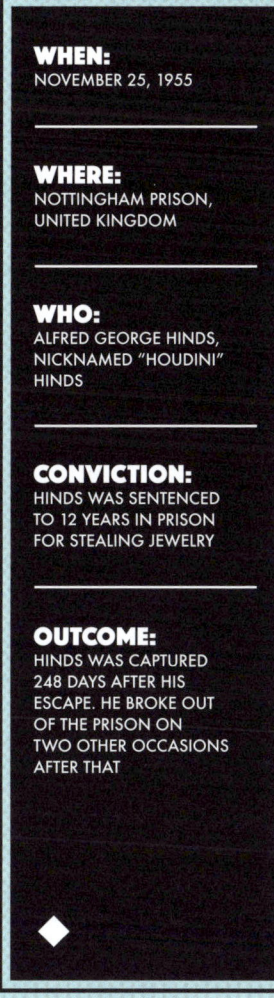

WHEN:
NOVEMBER 25, 1955

WHERE:
NOTTINGHAM PRISON,
UNITED KINGDOM

WHO:
ALFRED GEORGE HINDS,
NICKNAMED "HOUDINI"
HINDS

CONVICTION:
HINDS WAS SENTENCED
TO 12 YEARS IN PRISON
FOR STEALING JEWELRY

OUTCOME:
HINDS WAS CAPTURED
248 DAYS AFTER HIS
ESCAPE. HE BROKE OUT
OF THE PRISON ON
TWO OTHER OCCASIONS
AFTER THAT

BOOTY FROM THE ROBBERY AT THE MAPLES DEPARTMENT STORE, LONDON.

THE AUTHORITIES NEVER MANAGED TO RECOVER THE STOLEN JEWELS AND CASH

MINOR MISDEMEANORS

Alfred "Houdini" Hinds was born in London in 1917. Following the death of his father, Hinds was sent to an orphanage, where he developed his wiliness, which was undoubtedly one of his strongest assets.

Hinds committed various robberies even as a child. He escaped from the orphanage at the age of seven and was sent to a center for juvenile delinquents, from which he also managed to escape.

With few alternatives, Hinds enlisted during World War II. However, the rebellious Hinds's military career was far from honorable, and he opted for a life of crime instead.

JEWELERY ROBBERY

In 1953, Alfred "Houdini" Hinds was arrested and accused of a major jewelry robbery, although he always denied it. He was sentenced to 12 years in HM Nottingham Prison in central England.

PLANNING THE ESCAPE

HIS STREAK OF JAILBREAKS HAD ONLY JUST BEGUN: HINDS BECAME VERY FAMOUS FOR HIS ESCAPES

THE ART OF OBSERVING

The cunning Hinds spent the first two years of his jail sentence meticulously planning his escape from Nottingham Prison, located 125 miles north of London.

The prisoner observed the guards' routines and all possible escape routes.

HE DECIDED TO ESCAPE AT NIGHT BECAUSE THAT WAS WHEN THE GUARDS SLACKED OFF

Studying the guards' routines, he realized that there was hardly any surveillance in the prison at night. The astute and bold Hinds devised a strategy for overcoming all obstacles.

A GENIUS LOCKSMITH

Back then, the cells at Nottingham Prison did not have toilet facilities. Instead of going to the bathroom, prisoners had to use an aluminum bucket as a urinal. It was this bucket that opened the prison gates for Hinds.

THE SKILLFUL HINDS MEMORIZED THE GUARDS' KEY AND CREATED A PERFECT REPLICA USING A PIECE OF METAL

For his escape, Hinds sculpted an exact copy of his cell's key using the urinal's metal handle.

His photographic memory served him well, enabling him to precisely picture the key he would regularly see in the guards' hands.

THE BUCKET'S HANDLE HELPED HIM FIND A WAY TO FREEDOM.

THE ESCAPE IN STEPS

1. THE MASTER KEY

Alfred Hinds waited for nightfall before implementing his plan. He then opened his cell door using the duplicate key he had made.

Only two guards were in charge of the prison's security, and Hinds was able to walk the corridors undetected.

Much to his good fortune—and as strange as it may seem—the self-made key also worked to open other doors at the prison.

2. SCALING THE WALL

But there was still another huge obstacle for him to overcome—a 20-foot wall that separated him from freedom outside.

Once again, Alfred Hinds's ingenuity and skills saved his skin.

WITH HIM IN HIS ESCAPE WAS PATRICK FLEMING, A FELLOW PRISONER ALSO CONVICTED OF ROBBERY

He was able to get over the prison's high wall somehow, possibly using a rope he had made earlier or by stacking up pieces of wood from the carpentry workshop.

3. HIGHWAY ESCAPE

After jumping over a smaller wall and a wire fence, he made it out, where an accomplice was awaiting him in a car. From there, they fled to Dublin, Ireland, where he took refuge.

INVESTIGATION

The morning after the escape, the guards found Hinds's cell empty. The door was shut, and there was no sign of a jailbreak.

The staff at Nottingham Prison fell into a state of utter confusion. The guards simply couldn't understand what happened. How did the inmate get out? Where were his escape tools? The British press soon nicknamed him "Houdini" Hinds after the famous magician.

THE LEGENDARY ILLUSIONIST

HARRY HOUDINI

HARRY HOUDINI WAS FAMOUS IN THE UNITED STATES AND ACROSS EUROPE.

Harry Houdini (1874–1926), whose real name was Erik Weisz, was an Austro-Hungarian magician and escape artist who gained international fame for his truly breathtaking stunts.

Among his most acclaimed tricks were those relating to escapism. No matter how Harry Houdini was tied up, handcuffed, or otherwise trapped, he would always manage to free himself.

Nearly a century after his death, Houdini's legend lives on. That's why Hinds, a great artist of real-life jailbreaks, was promptly nicknamed after this iconic magician of history.

A NEW LIFE OUTSIDE

"Houdini" Hinds started a new life and career in Ireland, working as a builder and decorator, but he by no means flew under the radar. Instead he devoted himself to defending his innocence in the jewelry robbery.

Hinds constantly sent recordings and letters to the press and institutions, declaring his innocence and asking for a retrial.

HINDS'S REPEATED DECLARATIONS OF INNOCENCE FROM HIS HIDEOUT CATAPULTED HIM TO FAME

HINDS REPEATS HIS FEAT

THE SEEMINGLY IMPOSSIBLE HAPPENS AGAIN: "HOUDINI" DISAPPEARS DURING HIS TRIAL AT THE COURT OF JUSTICE

HE KNEW IT WAS EASIER TO ESCAPE FROM THE COURTHOUSE THAN FROM THE PRISON, AND SO HE FILED A COMPLAINT IN ORDER TO GET A HEARING

After 248 days at large, Hinds was caught by Scotland Yard in Dublin. His obsessive calls for justice took their toll—he was located, detained, and transferred back to London—but he soon escaped again.

PERMISSION TO GO TO THE BATHROOM

Everything was proceeding normally during Hinds's appearance before the High Court in London when he asked to go to the bathroom. The judge consented, and the prisoner left the room accompanied by two guards.

But an accomplice was waiting for him in the bathroom. Together, they chained up the surprised guards. Soon after, Hinds calmly left the building and took refuge on bustling Fleet Street, bound for Bristol airport.

AFTER BEING RECOGNIZED BY THE FLIGHT ATTENDANT ON BOARD A PLANE BOUND FOR DUBLIN, "HOUDINI" HINDS WAS SENT BY POLICE TO LONDON'S PENTONVILLE PRISON.

THE SHREWD HINDS SUED THE POLICE FOR ILLEGAL ARREST. HIS HEARING BEFORE THE JUDGE GAVE HIM A CHANCE TO ESCAPE FROM THE COURTHOUSE.

NEARLY FIVE HOURS AFTER HIS AMAZING ESCAPE, HINDS WAS IDENTIFIED ON BOARD A PLANE SHORTLY BEFORE TAKEOFF

ALBERT HINDS, ESCORTED BY A POLICE OFFICER, INSIDE A CAR TAKING HIM TO LONDON'S PENTONVILLE PRISON IN JUNE 1957.

THIRD & FINAL ESCAPE

ANOTHER FEAT

After his last escape was thwarted by a flight attendant when he had already boarded the plane, Hinds was sent to the United Kingdom's second high-security prison: Chelmsford.

But "Houdini" managed yet another jailbreak less than a year later, slipping out through the prison's laundry. He fled to Dublin, where he spent two years living under a false name before being discovered when driving a stolen car. He was sent back to prison.

OVER FOUR YEARS, HE ESCAPED FROM TWO HIGH-SECURITY PRISONS AND A COURTHOUSE

CHELMSFORD PRISON WAS FAMOUS FOR ITS FORTRESSLIKE SECURITY—NOBODY HAD EVER MANAGED TO ESCAPE FROM IT

FREEDOM

In 1964, Hinds finished his jail sentence and left prison. The popular "Houdini" then wrote a book recounting his extraordinary adventures.

Since his conviction, Hinds had turned himself into a veritable legal expert, and his criticisms and highlighting of flaws in the British legal system caused quite a sensation. People listened to him and his ideas, and Alfred Hinds finally found his place in the world.

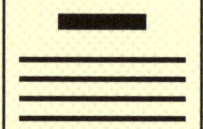

San Francisco Chronicle
THE VOICE OF THE WEST

FINAL

98th YEAR | **No. 162** | **CCCCAAA** | **TUESDAY, JUNE 12, 1962** | **10 CENTS** | **GArfield 1-1111**

THREE PRISONERS FLEE FROM "WORLD'S MOST SECURE PRISON"

THE GREAT ESCAPE FROM ALCATRAZ

UNTIL JUNE 11, 1962, NOBODY HAD MANAGED TO ESCAPE FROM THIS FORMIDABLE PRISON

THE FUGITIVES LEFT THE ISLAND ON A RAFT. IT IS STILL UNKNOWN WHETHER THEY MADE IT TO LAND.

WAS THIS THE PERFECT ESCAPE?

Armed robber Frank Morris and bank-robbing brothers John and Clarence Anglin were incarcerated at Alcatraz following attempted escapes at other US prisons.

Although it had been claimed that this famous jail was escape-proof, it took the trio only a few months to break out. Nobody knows, however, if they survived or drowned in the dangerous waters of the Pacific Ocean.

THE THREE ESCAPEES TOOK TO THE ROUGH WATERS OF THE PACIFIC IN A RAFT.

WHEN:	**WHERE:**	**WHO:**	**CONVICTION:**	**OUTCOME:**
THE NIGHT OF JUNE 11/12, 1962	ALCATRAZ FEDERAL PENITENTIARY, SAN FRANCISCO BAY, CALIFORNIA, USA (ALSO KNOWN AS THE ROCK)	FRANK MORRIS AND BROTHERS JOHN AND CLARENCE ANGLIN	THE THREE ESCAPEES WERE EACH SERVING SENTENCES OF MORE THAN 10 YEARS FOR ARMED ROBBERIES AND HOLDUPS AT VARIOUS BANKS	IN THE ABSENCE OF EVIDENCE OF THE ESCAPEES' SURVIVAL, THE POLICE DEEMED THEM TO HAVE DIED, DESPITE NEVER FINDING THEIR BODIES

AN IMPREGNABLE FORTRESS

This is the small rocky island of Alcatraz in the San Francisco Bay, California. It was chosen as the location for the most secure prison in the United States. The facility was built on rock, making it difficult, if not impossible, for escape tunnels to be dug.

MAIN BUILDING (CELLS)

SECURITY GATE

ALCATRAZ WAS A CORRECTIONAL FACILITY CAPABLE OF REHABILITATING EVEN THE MOST REBELLIOUS OF PRISONERS

1. LIGHTHOUSE
2. BAKER BEACH
3. PRISON DIRECTOR'S RESIDENCE
4. WALL
5. PARADE GROUND
6. GUARDHOUSE
7. RESIDENTIAL APARTMENTS
8. DOCK
9. OFFICERS' CLUB
10. POWER HOUSE
11. MODEL INDUSTRIES BUILDING
12. WATER TOWER
13. RECREATION YARD

BLOCK D
KITCHEN
CANTEEN
WARDEN'S HOUSE
BLOCK C
VISITORS' HALL
BLOCK B
BLOCK A
BARBER
DIRECTOR'S OFFICE
ENTRANCE

THE PRISON HAD FOUR BLOCKS AND ACCOMMODATED SOME 260 INMATES. ALMOST ALL OF THEM LIVED IN TINY INDIVIDUAL CELLS IN BLOCKS B AND C.

THE MOST FEARSOME PRISON

In 1934, it was decided that this gigantic prison would be turned into the "prison of all prisons." It was upgraded with electric fences, barbed wire, and hefty iron bars. Security was beefed up and strict rules were established, including a dozen daily inspections. It was to Alcatraz that the country's most dangerous criminals were sent.

THE SECURITY SYSTEM, WITH ONE WARDEN FOR EVERY THREE INMATES, WAS COPIED AT OTHER PRISONS

29 YEARS OF NONSTOP OPERATION

14 FOILED ESCAPE ATTEMPTS

36 PRISONERS WHO TRIED TO ESCAPE

PLANNING
THE ESCAPE

THE ESCAPEES' FORMIDABLE INGENUITY AND DEXTERITY WERE THE KEY TO THEIR SUCCESSFUL ESCAPE

POLICE MUG SHOTS OF THE THREE ESCAPEES, FRANK LEE MORRIS, CLARENCE ANGLIN, AND JOHN ANGLIN. THE ANGLIN BROTHERS LIVED IN ADJACENT CELLS, AS DID MORRIS AND A FOURTH PERSON INVOLVED IN THE ESCAPE, ALLEN WEST (WHO DID NOT END UP ACTUALLY ESCAPING).

THE LONG ROUTE TO FREEDOM

The prisoners spent their days locked up in their own tiny cells, in strict silence. Morris and the Anglin brothers started plotting their escape in hushed whispers. Car thief Allen West was involved in their plans, although he did not end up escaping with them.

THE PRISONERS WERE ALLOWED TO TALK ONLY DURING BRIEF BREAKS AT THE WEEKEND

ESCAPE HOLE

It all started when one of the inmates found some old saw blades, which were then used to build a makeshift drill (making use of the motor of a broken vacuum cleaner).

With the help of the drill, a 10-cent coin, a few stolen spoons, and other tools they managed to get hold of, the prisoners achieved their first objective—to loosen the air-duct grate in each of their cells and to enlarge the ventilation hole to find out where it led.

The air duct was in the back wall of the cells. Since the Anglins lived in adjacent cells, just like Morris and West, they worked in pairs—one would work and the other would keep watch.

The inmates also took advantage of the jail's musical activity hours to get the noisiest work done.

TO HIDE THE ENLARGED HOLE, THEY COVERED IT WITH A PIECE OF CARDBOARD PAINTED AT THE WORKSHOP TO LOOK LIKE THE WALL AND THE GRATE

NIGHTTIME OUTINGS

Once the air-duct hole was sufficiently wide enough for them to slip inside, the inmates began their late-night outings, exploring the corridor behind the duct and its surrounds and starting to plan their escape route.

Once everything was in place, they chose their escape date—the night of June 11.

THEY PUT DUMMY HEADS IN THEIR BEDS WHENEVER THEY LEFT THEIR CELLS TO PREPARE FOR THE ESCAPE

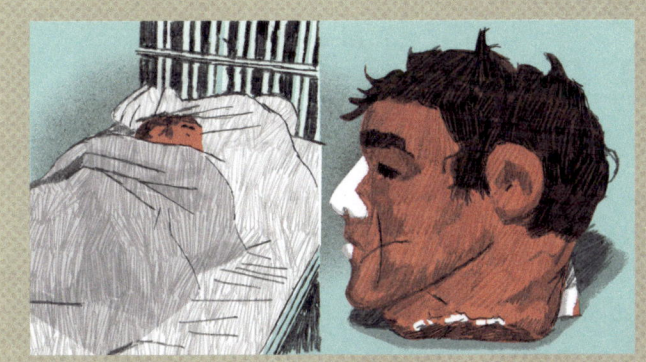

A CLANDESTINE WORKSHOP

During one of their outings, they discovered an area that had no security surveillance, and so they turned it into a workshop/storeroom.

It took them several months to create the objects they needed to execute their plan:

1.
DUMMY HEADS

They made dummy heads from papier-mâché, with locks of real hair stolen from the barbershop.

2.
LIFE VESTS AND INFLATABLE RAFT

The prisoners made a raft with more than 50 raincoats, some of which were bought, others gifted or stolen.

3.
RAFT AIR PUMP

They created this using the remains of an old musical instrument they had discovered.

4.
WOODEN PADDLES

One was found at the prison and another on Angel Island.

---

5 FEET

9 FEET

8 FEET

AIR VENT   SHELVES

FOLDING TABLE

UNBREAKABLE STEEL BARS

THE CELLS WERE IN FULL VIEW. THEY WERE 5 FEET WIDE, 9 FEET LONG, AND 8 FEET HIGH, WITH A SMALL SINK AND A TOILET ON THE REAR WALL.

THE ESCAPE IN STEPS

ONE OF THE ESCAPEES EMERGES FROM THE AIR DUCT ON THE ROOF OF THE BUILDING.

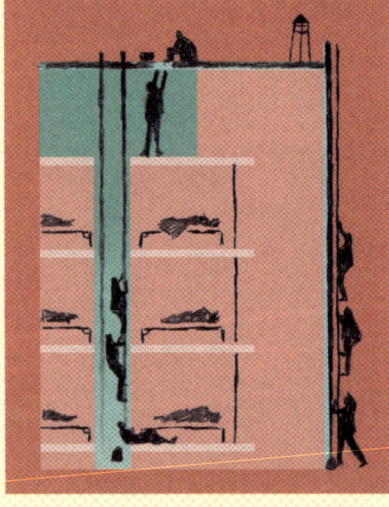

1. LEAVING THE CELLS

After a final bed check at 9 p. m., Morris and the Anglins left their cells via the air-duct holes.

That was the moment at which Allen West stayed behind. It is unknown whether he was actually unable to escape or was simply paralyzed with fear. The others took all their prepared equipment and made their way up to the roof.

THE GUARDS HEARD A LOUD NOISE AS THE INMATES WERE EMERGING FROM THE AIR DUCT, BUT NOT HEARING ANYTHING MORE, THEY DIDN'T THINK IT WAS IMPORTANT

2. DESTINATION: THE OCEAN

They crept along the roof, undetected by the spotlights, before sliding 50 feet down a pipe on an outside wall to the ground and running to the barbed wire fence surrounding the complex. They jumped over the fence and headed down an embankment to the northern shore of Alcatraz Island—this was probably at around 11 p. m.

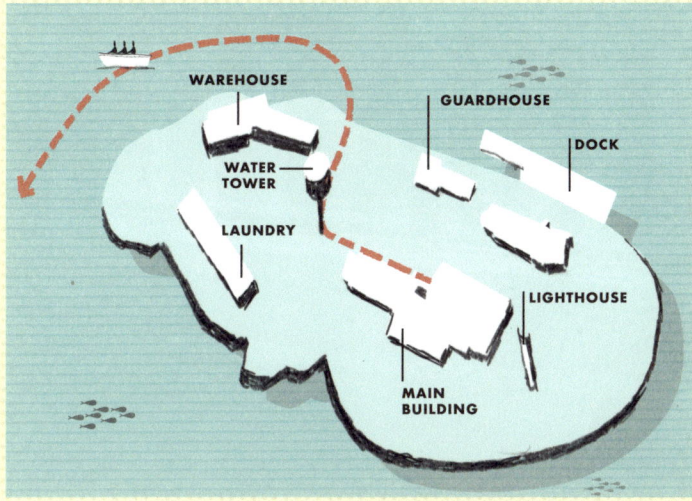

THE ESCAPE ROUTE FROM THE CELL BLOCK TO THE OCEAN.

3. THE RAFT

This was the point at which the escapees faced one of the biggest hurdles to their escape from Alcatraz. They would have to cross about a mile of shark-infested waters, featuring dangerous currents, which separated the island of Alzatraz from US mainland.

And the darkness further complicated matters. They put all their materials to the test.

The raft and improvised life vests appear to have worked. In the cold dead of night, Morris and the Anglin brothers rowed with all their might to flee the "world's most secure prison."

THEY INFLATED THE RAFT USING THEIR HOMEMADE PUMP AND SET OFF INTO THE PACIFIC

ONCE ON THE ROOF OF THE PRISON, THE ESCAPEES CRAWLED TO THE FAR END OF THE BUILDING, AVOIDING THE SPOTLIGHTS, AND SCALED DOWN ONE OF THE EXTERIOR WALLS.

THE INVESTIGATION

THE POLICE SEARCHED ALL THE NEARBY ISLANDS AND FOUND SOME TRACES OF THE ESCAPEES, BUT IT IS UNCLEAR WHETHER THEY DROWNED OR SURVIVED.

OFFICERS DISCOVERED THE THREE EMPTY CELLS DURING THE FIRST CHECK OF THE MORNING

ALCATRAZ ON ALERT

The three wily prisoners managed to escape from Alcatraz by leaving papier-mache heads in their beds to trick the night guards into believing that they were still in their cells.

A loud siren immediately started blaring from the top of "The Rock," and an intense pursuit began. Police, federal agents, the coast guard, dogs, and army helicopters all combed the island and the San Francisco coast.

DEAD OR ALIVE?

While most reports support the theory that the escapees drowned or were eaten by sharks, their bodies were never located. Later, a paddle was found on Angel Island, the largest island in the bay, which may have been one of their planned stops.

The people in charge at Alcatraz eventually proclaimed the three escapees dead, and the FBI closed the case of the famous escape in 1979.

AFTER THEIR INGENIOUS JAILBREAK WITHOUT ANY HELP, THEY BECAME THE MOST WANTED AND FAMOUS CRIMINALS IN THE COUNTRY

THE LEGEND LIVES ON

JOHN ANGLIN,
THE STRANGE LETTER

Half a century after the case was finally closed, the Richmond police department in California received a letter supposedly written by John Anglin. In it, he said:

I escaped from Alcatraz in June 1962 with my brother Clarence and Frank Morris. I'm 83 years old and in bad shape. I have cancer. Yes we all made it that night but barely!

The FBI was not able to verify if the letter was genuine, but it was never proven to be fake. The mystery of the great escape from Alcatraz continues.

"YES WE ALL MADE IT THAT NIGHT BUT BARELY!"

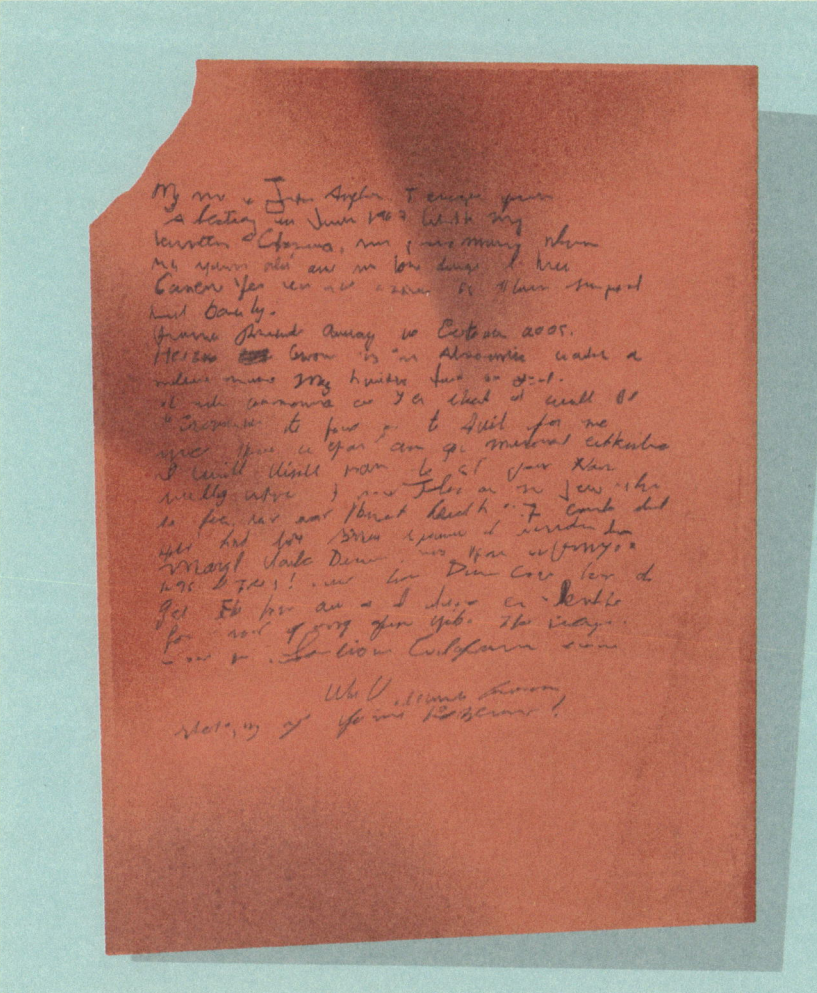

THE END OF ALCATRAZ

Alcatraz closed its doors just a few months after the escape following the **stunning security oversight** mostly because of the high cost of maintaining the prison.

LEGENDARY PRISONERS

More than 1,500 inmates spent time on The Rock, including famous **bank robbers, counterfeiters, mobsters, and even bloodthirsty murderers.** The notorious gangster Al Capone spent four years at Alcatraz. Another famous prisoner was Robert Stroud, the Birdman, who spent his jail time studying and caring for canaries.

THE FILM

Six months before the federal agents closed the case, the movie *Escape From Alcatraz* (1979) was released, directed by Don Siegel, starring Clint Eastwood, and inspired by the story.

EL PAÍS

YEAR LII- NO. 19.183   MONTEVIDEO, FRIDAY, JULY 30, 1971   32-PAGE EDITION

FOUNDING DIRECTOR: EDUARDO RODRÍGUEZ LARRETA   PRICE: $20.30

JAILBREAK FROM WOMEN'S PRISON VIA TUNNEL

THE FEMALE FUGITIVES CRAWLED THROUGH A TUNNEL TO ESCAPE FROM CABILDO PRISON IN MONTEVIDEO, URUGUAY. THE ESCAPE WAS ORGANIZED EXTERNALLY BY THE PRISONERS' BUDDIES, SINCE THEY WERE ALL PART OF THE TUPAMAROS URBAN GUERILLA GROUP.

OPERATION STAR: ESCAPE OF 38 WOMEN

THE FEMALE PRISONERS CREPT DOWN A TUNNEL TO THE SEWERS, THEN TO A NEIGHBORING HOUSE

WHEN:	WHERE:	WHO:	CONVICTION:	OUTCOME:
THE NIGHT OF JULY 30, 1971	CABILDO PRISON, MONTEVIDEO, URUGUAY	38 WOMEN PRISONERS OF THE MLN-T	VARIOUS CONVICTIONS FOR BELONGING TO URUGUAY'S TUPAMAROS URBAN GUERILLA GROUP	THE 38 FUGITIVES MANAGED TO ESCAPE, BUT MOST OF THEM WERE ARRESTED AGAIN OVER TIME

OUTSIDE HELP

A group of 38 female prisoners escaped from Cabildo women's prison in Montevideo. They belonged to the *Movimiento de Liberación Nacional-Tupamaros* (National Liberation Movement, MLN-T), ideologically on the far left, and acted as an urban guerrilla group throughout the 1960s and early '70s. The people of Uruguay were starving, and the Tupamaros intended to challenge the government.

A SECRET OPERATION

The head of the Tupamaros masterminded the escape, code-named *Operación Estrella* (Operation Star), from outside the prison.

Communication with the prisoners group members was by a clever numerical code. During visits, family members would pass coded messages on rolled-up cigarette paper to the inmates. They called these "pills" and hid them in their mouths. The prisoners decoded the messages to prepare for their escape. They also received miniature pencil-drawn plans.

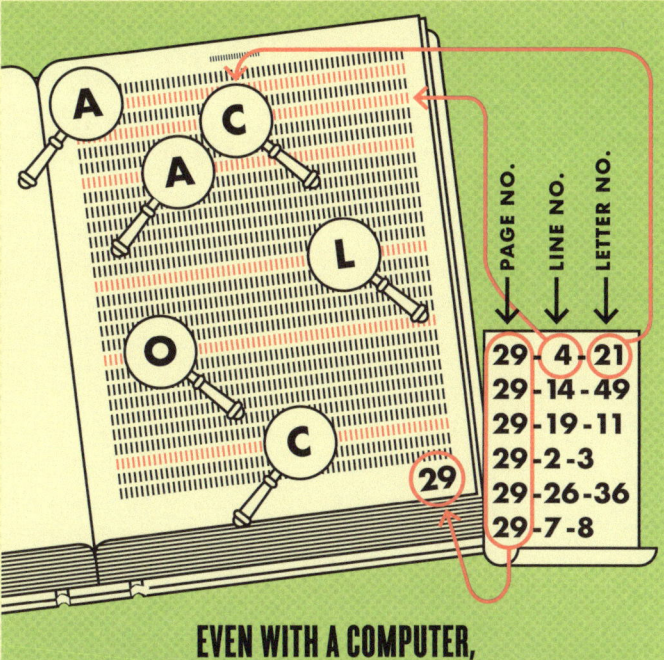

A SECRET CODE WAS USED TO INDICATE LETTERS IN A PARTICULAR BOOK. THE PRISONERS WERE GIVEN A PAGE, LINE, AND LETTER NUMBER. THEY COULD FORM WORDS FOLLOWING A SEQUENCE OF CODES. USING THE REAL CODES PICTURED HERE, WE CAN DECODE THE SPANISH WORD FOR "SEWER": C-L-O-A-C-A.

PAGE NO.   LINE NO.   LETTER NO.

29	4	21
29	14	49
29	19	11
29	2	3
29	26	36
29	7	8

EVEN WITH A COMPUTER, IT WAS IMPOSSIBLE TO DECODE THE MESSAGES WITHOUT KNOWING WHICH BOOK WAS USED

CABILDO PRISON WAS A WOMEN'S JAIL. AT THE TIME OF THE ESCAPE, IT HELD 43 INMATES, ALL OF WHOM BELONGED TO THE TUPAMAROS MOVEMENT.

THE TUPAMAROS'S SYMBOL, A STAR, INSPIRED THE NAME OF THE ESCAPE PLAN: OPERATION STAR.

PLANNING THE DETAIL

THEY PLANNED TO USE A SECTION OF THE CITY'S SEWER NETWORK AND HAVE THE PRISONERS EMERGE ONTO A STREET NOT FAR FROM THE PRISON

A year before the Operation Star escape, Cabildo had been the scene of another high-profile jailbreak, similarly orchestrated by Tupamaro inmates.

THE 13 "DOVES"

A group of 13 women from the MLN-T escaped during the prison's daily Mass.

Until then, nuns from the Buen Pastor Convent had been in charge of security at Cabildo Prison, but it was now decided to use female police officers.

As a result of the beefed-up security, the Tupamaros decided to opt for an underground jailbreak for their 38 women members.

STOLEN MAPS

The planners discovered that the sewer network in the prison's vicinity was very old and that the pipes were wide enough to move through. Using maps stolen from the Montevideo city hall, the Tupamaros were able to trace a route running beneath the city.

It took them five months of work to plot the escape and to perfect coordination between the inmates and the external group.

> **THE IMPRISONED TUPAMARO GUERRILLAS AND THEIR COUNTERPARTS OUTSIDE THE PRISON WORKED AS A TEAM**

FROM THE OUTSIDE IN

The plan was to act from the outside in. The external group members had rented a house several streets from the prison. Inside, they drilled a tunnel that connected to the municipal sewer network.

The route to Calle Acevedo Díaz via the sewer pipes stretched belowground for several blocks. Once there, they dug another tunnel to connect the sewers with one of the residential wings in the prison building.

> **THE PRISONERS MEASURED THE FLOOR OF THEIR DORMITORY AND MARKED EXACTLY WHERE THE TUNNEL OPENING WOULD BE**

Calle Acevedo Díaz

Calle Hocquart

RENTED HOUSE
(BEGINNING AND END OF THE ESCAPE ROUTE)

Calle Constitución

WOMEN'S PRISON
(CALLE CABILDO, CORNER OF CALLE NICARAGUA)

SEWER ROUTE   TUNNEL ROUTE

THE UNDERGROUND ROUTE THAT THE WOMEN FOLLOWED ON THEIR WAY TO FREEDOM, AIDED BY THEIR FELLOW GROUP MEMBERS WHO HAD COME TO MEET THEM.

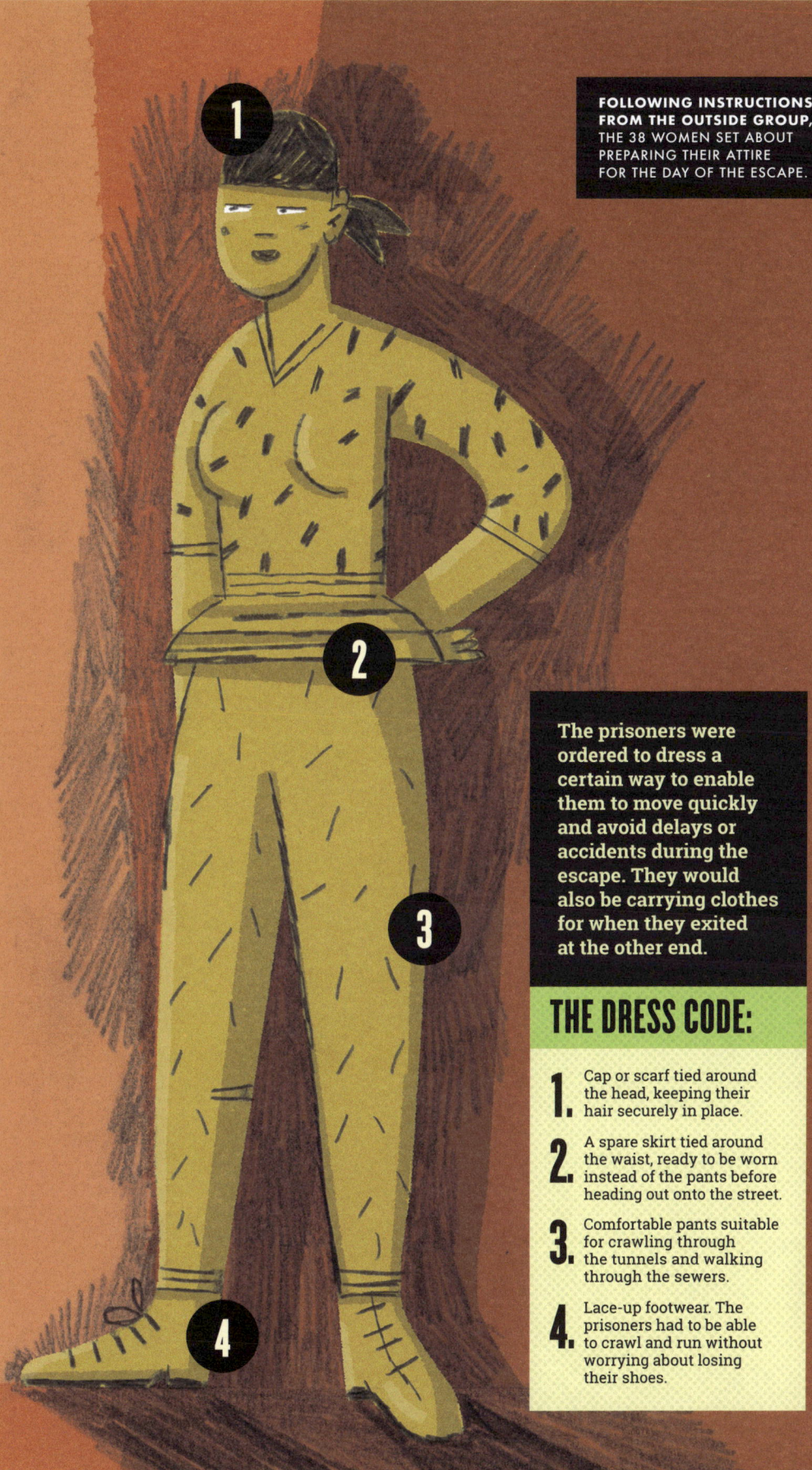

FOLLOWING INSTRUCTIONS FROM THE OUTSIDE GROUP, THE 38 WOMEN SET ABOUT PREPARING THEIR ATTIRE FOR THE DAY OF THE ESCAPE.

The prisoners were ordered to dress a certain way to enable them to move quickly and avoid delays or accidents during the escape. They would also be carrying clothes for when they exited at the other end.

THE DRESS CODE:

1. Cap or scarf tied around the head, keeping their hair securely in place.

2. A spare skirt tied around the waist, ready to be worn instead of the pants before heading out onto the street.

3. Comfortable pants suitable for crawling through the tunnels and walking through the sewers.

4. Lace-up footwear. The prisoners had to be able to crawl and run without worrying about losing their shoes.

TOP SECRET

To prevent Operation Star from being discovered, only the high-ranking prisoners were informed of the plans. The remaining prison inmates found out about it only a few days before the actual escape.

When it was finally time to tell everyone, most agreed to the plan. It was a difficult decision for them to make because, if they did manage to escape, they would be condemned to a life in hiding for the rest of their days.

ONLY FIVE OF THE PRISONERS CHOSE TO STAY IN THE PRISON

MASKING THE NOISE

As the tunnel diggers got closer to the dormitory floor, the prisoners had to invent ways of masking the noise of the drilling, so they pretended to fight, they sang, they laughed heartily, they organized parties …

THEY USED ANY EXCUSE TO MAKE A RACKET AND CONCEAL THE NOISE CAUSED BY THOSE DIGGING THEIR ESCAPE TUNNEL

THE ESCAPE IN STEPS

1. THE START SIGNAL

On July 30, 1971, everything was in place. The fellow group members who dug the tunnel from the outside had finally reached the prison floor inside.

It was agreed that the women would wait until nightfall before opening the access hole on the dormitory floor.

At around 10 p. m., after the guards' final inspection, the accomplices gave three knocks on the floor and the prisoners responded to the signal.

THE KNOCKS MARKED THE START OF OPERATION STAR

2. LAST-MINUTE PREPARATIONS

The inmates used various items in their cells to make it look like they were in bed and fast asleep. Meanwhile, the outside group members in the tunnel drilled through the floor.

THE 38 WOMEN PRISONERS EQUIPPED THEMSELVES AS AGREED

It was important for the women to tie the skirts around their waists; these would be swapped for their dirty pants, which they would leave behind after the escape, so that they wouldn't be recognized when they moved around outside.

ONE BY ONE, THE WOMEN DISAPPEARED INTO THE TUNNEL, AND THE PRISON DORMITORY GRADUALLY EMPTIED OUT.

3. ENTERING THE TUNNEL

One by one, the inmates sneaked into the tunnel in the order they had previously agreed on. The women in the worst physical condition would leave first; those with the longest prison sentences would be last.

Their fellow group members were waiting for them underground, ready to guide them to freedom.

DURING THE MINUTES BEFORE FLEEING, THE PRISONERS USED PILLOWS, PAJAMAS, AND OTHER ITEMS OF CLOTHING TO CREATE DUMMIES THAT LOOKED AS IF THEY WERE ASLEEP IN THEIR BEDS.

4. JOURNEY THROUGH THE SEWERS

The female guerrillas and their fellow MLN-T buddies crawled their way around the odorous, rat-infested sewage system. They split into separate groups, each with a guide, and used flashlights for light in what was otherwise total darkness.

The organizers had thought of just about everything—they left a trail of false leads behind them, to throw the police off and to protect the identity of the people whom they had rented the house from.

THEY PRETENDED TO HAVE ESCAPED VIA THE SECTION OF SEWERS LEADING TO THE SEA

The Tupamaros had sealed the lids covering the openings into the sewers from the sidewalk with wire to avoid being cornered by the police in the event of problems.

OTHER MEMBERS OF THE ORGANIZATION HELPED THEM OUT OF THE TUNNEL AND INTO THE HOUSE.

5. THE HOUSE

Within the space of a few hours, all the women and the entire rescue group had managed to leave the prison and reach the house or "center of operations."

Other members of the organization waited for them at the house, giving the women weapons, money, and false ID documents to successfully complete the escape.

THERE WAS A TREMENDOUS SENSE OF JOY, BUT THEY HAD TO KEEP CALM BECAUSE THEY WEREN'T SAFE YET

A PERFECT, METICULOUSLY PREPARED ESCAPE

51 INCHES
WAS THE HEIGHT OF THE SEWER PIPE

47 INCHES
WAS THE HEIGHT OF THE TUNNELS

2 TUNNELS HAD TO BE DUG

5 MONTHS—TIME IT TOOK TO PREPARE FOR THE ESCAPE

2 HOURS—TIME IT TOOK TO REACH THE HOUSE

6. HIGHWAY ESCAPE

During the days before the escape, the Tupamaros parked several cars in the garage adjacent to the house.

In the early hours of the escape morning, the 38 women prisoners were driven to various parts of Montevideo, where they stayed undercover with fellow group members. The plan worked perfectly.

THE ESCAPEES ARRIVED IN THE BEDROOM OF THE RENTED HOUSE ONE BY ONE. SOME STARTED CELEBRATING THEIR SUCCESS, BUT A FELLOW GROUP MEMBER REMINDED THEM THAT ANY NOISE MIGHT GIVE THEM AWAY.

POLICE INVESTIGATION & FREEDOM

UNDERCOVER

Later that morning, the alarm was raised at the prison, and the escape was on the front page of every newspaper in Uruguay.

The police search for the fugitives in the sewer network began immediately, but the prisoners had long left and were hiding out for a while, and even after that time, they continued living clandestine lives.

They were almost all recaptured over the next two years and served long sentences under conditions much harsher than those at Cabildo Prison.

AMNESTY

When the dictatorship in Uruguay ended in 1985, all the imprisoned MLN-T members were freed under the Amnesty Law (they were pardoned).

Two senior members of the Tupamaros, Pepe Mujica and Lucía Topolansky, became the president and vice president of Uruguay, respectively. Lucía was one of the 38 women escapees.

IT TOOK THE POLICE SEVERAL MONTHS TO WORK OUT HOW THE ESCAPE HAD BEEN CARRIED OUT

IN THEIR SEARCH FOR THE ESCAPED PRISONERS, THE LAW-ENFORCEMENT AGENCIES SCOURED THE SEWERS OF MONTEVIDEO, BUT THEY DIDN'T FIND THEM.

TUPAMARO PRISONERS CELEBRATE THEIR FREEDOM AS DEMOCRACY RETURNED TO URUGUAY.

today
EUROPE
AND DIE WELT

DIE 🌐 WELT
INDEPENDENT DAILY FOR GERMANY

From man on the moon to successful manager
Page 4

Sunday, September 16, 1979

No. 216 Price 38 Pf

FLEEING THE GDR IN A BALLOON!

TWO FAMILIES ESCAPE FROM EAST GERMANY, THANKS TO HOT AIR

THEY MANAGED TO ESCAPE TO THE WESTERN HALF OF GERMANY BY CROSSING THE BORDER HIGH UP IN THE SKY

AN ENORMOUS HOT-AIR BALLOON, WHICH THE FAMILIES MADE THEMSELVES, HELPED THEM CROSS THE DANGEROUS, HEAVILY GUARDED BORDER.

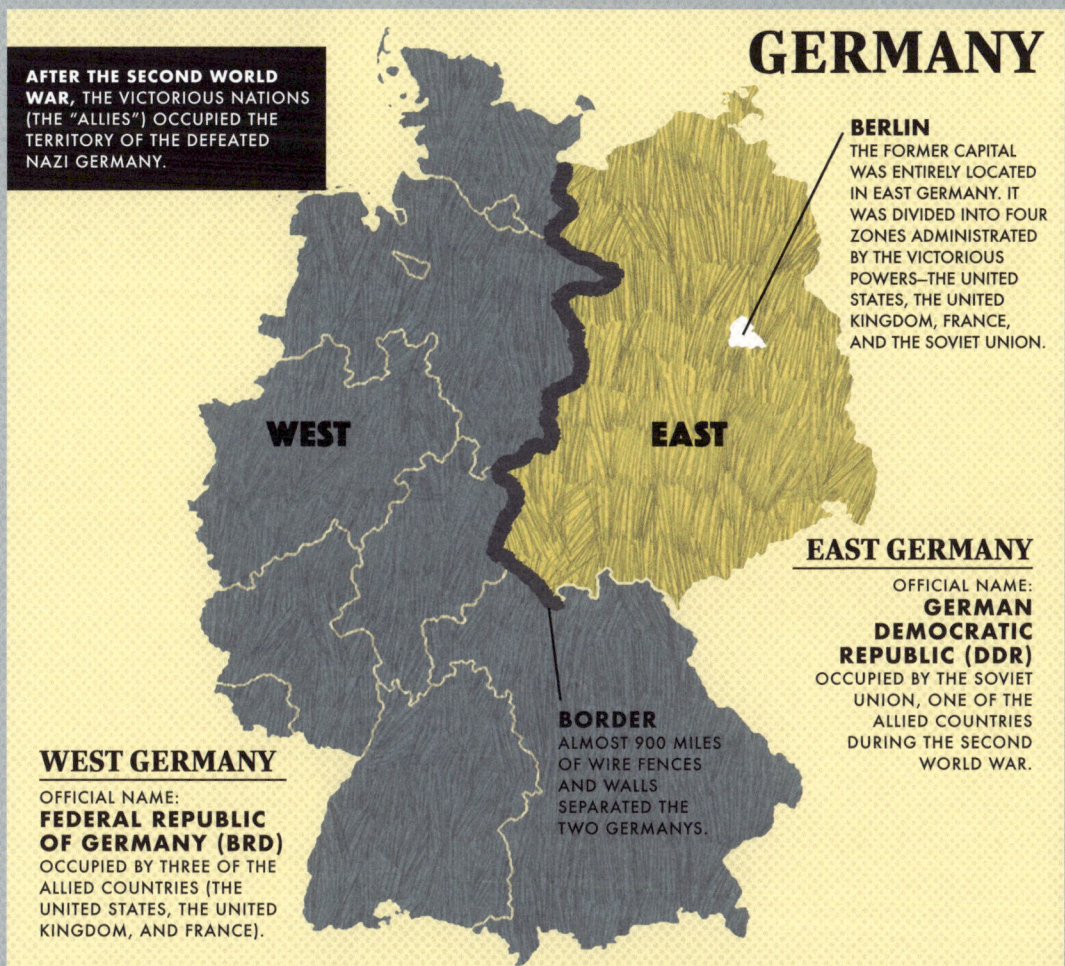

GERMANY

AFTER THE SECOND WORLD WAR, THE VICTORIOUS NATIONS (THE "ALLIES") OCCUPIED THE TERRITORY OF THE DEFEATED NAZI GERMANY.

WEST

EAST

BERLIN
THE FORMER CAPITAL WAS ENTIRELY LOCATED IN EAST GERMANY. IT WAS DIVIDED INTO FOUR ZONES ADMINISTRATED BY THE VICTORIOUS POWERS—THE UNITED STATES, THE UNITED KINGDOM, FRANCE, AND THE SOVIET UNION.

EAST GERMANY
OFFICIAL NAME:
GERMAN DEMOCRATIC REPUBLIC (DDR)
OCCUPIED BY THE SOVIET UNION, ONE OF THE ALLIED COUNTRIES DURING THE SECOND WORLD WAR.

BORDER
ALMOST 900 MILES OF WIRE FENCES AND WALLS SEPARATED THE TWO GERMANYS.

WEST GERMANY
OFFICIAL NAME:
FEDERAL REPUBLIC OF GERMANY (BRD)
OCCUPIED BY THREE OF THE ALLIED COUNTRIES (THE UNITED STATES, THE UNITED KINGDOM, AND FRANCE).

WHEN:
SEPTEMBER 16, 1979

WHERE:
PÖSSNECK—A CITY IN THE FEDERAL STATE OF THURINGIA, EAST GERMANY

WHO:
THE WETZEL AND STRELZYK FAMILIES

CONVICTION:
NONE. THEY FLED EAST GERMANY, WHERE FREEDOM WAS SEVERELY RESTRICTED.

OUTCOME:
THEY MANAGED TO ESCAPE ACROSS THE BORDER BY AIR, LANDING NEAR NAILA, IN THE FEDERAL STATE OF BAVARIA, WEST GERMANY.

A DIVIDED GERMANY

The allied forces that emerged victorious from the Second World War (1939–1945) occupied Germany, which was defeated and devastated by bombings. The United States, the United Kingdom, France, and the Soviet Union (present-day Russia), split the country into four zones.

A CLOSED BORDER

The zones were initially intended to be temporary, and during the first few years, it was indeed possible to cross the border between West Germany (occupied by the Americans, British, and French) and East Germany (occupied by the Soviets). But the ongoing conflict between East and West made reunification of the two Germanys impossible.

One night in August 1961, with no prior warning, the GDR closed the border between the two Germanys. East Germans were suddenly no longer able to travel to the West.

Walls and watchtowers were erected and wire fences put in place. East German soldiers stopped or shot anyone trying to cross the border.

THOUSANDS OF PEOPLE TRIED TO ESCAPE THE GDR, RISKING THEIR LIVES TO REUNITE WITH THEIR LOVED ONES ON THE OTHER SIDE OF THE BORDER

ACROSS GERMANY AND IN BERLIN, THE BORDER WAS DEMARCATED BY A WALL THAT SPLIT THE ENTIRE COUNTRY IN TWO, SEPARATING MANY FAMILIES.

THE PROTAGONISTS

A MAGAZINE ARTICLE …

Günter Wetzel was one of the thousands upon thousands of Germans who were left isolated from the rest of the world in the GDR when the wall was built. He lived with his family in Pössneck, a small town in East Germany, 12 miles from the border with the West. He made a decent living as a builder.

TWO FRIENDS

In 1978, Wetzel's sister-in-law who lived in the West came to visit. Among other things, she brought along an old magazine with a feature on a hot-air balloon festival in the United States.

Günter Wetzel shared the article with his friend Peter Strelzyk, an electrician and former air force mechanic. Together, the two men came up with an idea …

GÜNTER AND PETER SET ABOUT BUILDING A HOT-AIR BALLOON TO ESCAPE WITH THEIR FAMILIES

TWO FAMILIES—EIGHT FUGITIVES

Günter and Petra Wetzel had two young children: Peter, age 5, and Andreas, just 2 years old. Peter Strelzyk and his wife, Doris, also had two children, albeit slightly older: Frank was 15, and Andreas 11 years old.

The STRELZYK Family
1. DORIS
2. ANDREAS
3. PETER
4. FRANK

The WETZEL Family
1. PETER
2. ANDREAS
3. PETRA
4. GÜNTER

DESIGNING IT

Before starting to build the hot-air balloon, the two men studied library books on mechanics, engineering, and physics. Both were skilled tinkerers and felt perfectly capable of taking on the challenge they had set themselves.

LIKE OTHER CITIZENS OF EAST GERMANY, PETER AND GÜNTER HAD OFTEN DISCUSSED ESCAPING THEIR COUNTRY BUT COULD NEVER WORK OUT HOW— UNTIL THEY CAME UP WITH THE BALLOON IDEA

THE RISK OF BEING FOUND OUT

The situation in the GDR at the time was very complicated. Many people in East Germany spied on their neighbors, friends, and even family members and informed the authorities. It was virtually impossible to know for certain whom one could trust.

Yet both Peter's wife (Doris) and Günter's (Petra) agreed to the plan, and both families started working in their basement. The entire operation had to remain top secret.

MAKING THE HOT-AIR BALLOON

LET'S DO THIS

Once they had worked out the balloon's design, the men set out to find the right material to build it.

The two families bought their fabrics and other parts they needed at a number of different stores so as not to raise the suspicions of the secret police (the Stasi). What they bought was not professional quality, but it would have to do.

THEY HAD TO STITCH NEARLY 14,000 SQ FT OF FABRIC PIECES TOGETHER FOR THE BALLOON

THE BALLOON

They made the fabric part of the balloon from silk, sheets, and remnants of tents and umbrellas, using a manual sewing machine and heavy-duty thread.

THE BURNER AND BASKET

The burner was constructed from a propane-gas tank connected to a valve, which enabled them to control the released gas and flames.

The basket was made out of a steel plate welded to several poles, which were connected with braided ropes.

NUMEROUS ATTEMPTS

To finish, they connected the basket to the fabric using nylon cords stitched over 48 vertical seams. All done!

They started testing the balloon, but it had several defects, and they had to have several goes before they were satisfied with the result.

THE BALLOON IN FULL FLIGHT, WITH THE WETZELS AND STRELZYKS ON BOARD.

THE ESCAPE IN STEPS

THEY SET OFF ON THEIR ESCAPE ON THE MORNING OF SEPTEMBER 16, 1979

1. THE CHOSEN LOCATION

Following several days of bad weather, at last there was a night when meteorological conditions were suitable for flying. Some time after midnight, the two families loaded the balloon parts into a car and drove to the location they had chosen for their escape—the tallest hill near their hometown of Pössneck.

Once they arrived in a clearing, they confirmed that the wind was perfect for their flight.

BEFORE UNLOADING THE BALLOON, THEY MADE SURE THAT NOBODY HAD FOLLOWED THEM

2. THE ASSEMBLY

At around 1:30 a. m., they set about quickly assembling the balloon, securing it to the ground with ropes. Using a fan, they managed to fully inflate the balloon within only five minutes. The escapees were ready to go!

The two families got in and started the burner. Soon after, the basket took off. The two men cut the anchoring ropes and ...

FILLED WITH EMOTION AND NERVES, THEY WATCHED AS THE BALLOON LIFTED OFF THE GROUND AND THEY TOOK FLIGHT

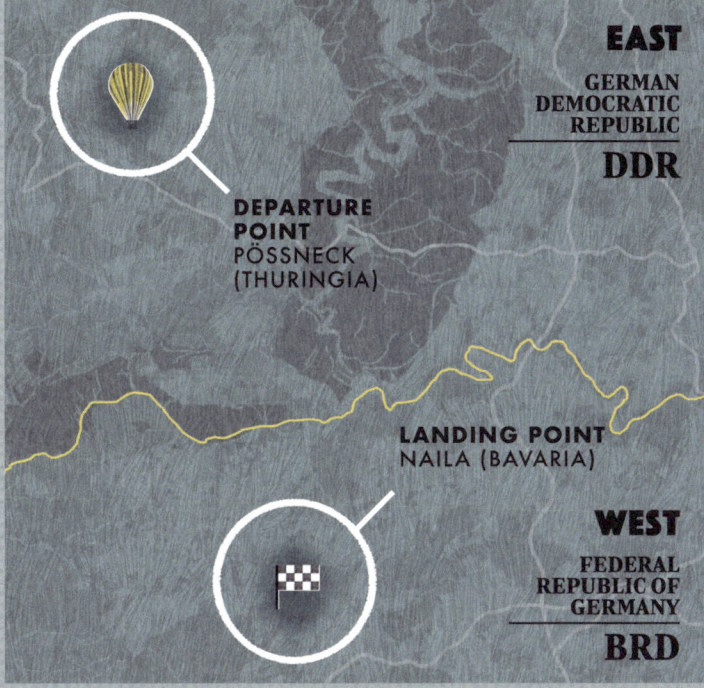

EAST
GERMAN DEMOCRATIC REPUBLIC
DDR

DEPARTURE POINT
PÖSSNECK (THURINGIA)

LANDING POINT
NAILA (BAVARIA)

WEST
FEDERAL REPUBLIC OF GERMANY
BRD

3. THE ASCENT

The basket wobbled, causing a small fire that they put out with an extinguisher. One of the anchoring ropes hit young Frank in the face, although the injury was minor. But worst of all, there was a hole in the balloon! To make up for this, the burner would have to be lit the whole time.

Despite all this, the balloon reached an altitude of 6,500 feet. A strong wind was blowing and they moved fast, enduring temperatures of barely 15°F.

The escapees kept the balloon burner running until it went out 20 minutes later. They had run out of gas!

THE FINAL PREPARATIONS. THE ESCAPEES STARTED THE BURNER AND AFTER CUTTING THE ANCHORING ROPES, THEY WERE READY TO GO!

SAFE AND SOUND. BOTH FAMILIES MANAGED TO GET OUT OF THE BASKET IN ONE PIECE, ALTHOUGH FRANK STRELZYK GOT HURT. INCREDIBLY, THEY DID NOT SUFFER ANY SERIOUS INJURIES.

4. THE DESCENT

They gradually started losing altitude, but once the balloon's air totally cooled, the descent became rather fast and got out of control.

The eight passengers huddled together, bracing for a dangerous landing. They could barely see where they were going and ended up crashing into some trees.

THE IMPACT WAS FIERCE BUT NOBODY WAS SERIOUSLY INJURED. THEY WERE ALL SAFE AND SOUND!

5. ON SOLID GROUND

They didn't know where they were, but they started heading south in the hope that they had reached West Germany.

SURVIVING THE FLIGHT WAS A GREAT FEAT IN ITSELF, BUT THEY STILL DIDN'T KNOW IF THEY HAD CROSSED THE BORDER

The signs they saw on their way didn't look familiar, and the tractor they came across was not made in East Germany.

So they had actually made it! They could hardly believe it.

FREE!

THE EIGHT HAD MANAGED TO CROSS THE BORDER. THEY WERE IN THE WEST!

The Strelzyk and Wetzel families had landed in a field near the small town of Naila (in the West German state of Bavaria). They were six miles from the border between East and West Germany.

The escapees had left the GDR behind, flying over its formidable border, its walls, death strip, land mines, and wire fences. They were utterly overjoyed!

HOW DID EAST AND WEST REACT TO THE ESCAPE?

A NEW LIFE

The escapees told the police that they had escaped East Germany for ideological reasons. They were issued West German passports and began their new lives in the Federal Republic.

THEY WROTE ONE OF THE MOST EMOTIONAL PAGES IN THE HISTORY OF THE TWO GERMANYS

The Wetzels soon refused to make any more media appearances, so the Strelzyks ended up getting all the attention.

TRAITORS OR HEROES?

East Germany labeled the eight escapees "traitors and enemies of the state," while in West Germany they were considered and even celebrated as veritable heroes.

MEDIA BONANZA IN THE WEST

In the West, articles about the Strelzyk and Wetzel families' daredevil escape were published in many newspapers. The families were interviewed and became well-known personalities.

THE FILM

Three years after the escape, Walt Disney Productions brought the story to the big screen with the movie *Night Crossing*, 1982, starring John Hurt (Peter Strelzyk) and Beau Bridges (Günter Wetzel).

THE TWO FRIENDS, GÜNTER WETZEL AND PETER STRELZYK, HAPPILY SHOWING OFF THEIR NEW WEST GERMAN PASSPORTS.

KOREA JOONGANG DAILY

Monday, September 17, 2012   **Your Window to Korea**   koreajoongangdaily.com

A PRISONER VANISHES THROUGH A MEAL-TRAY SLOT

YOGI-STYLE ESCAPE

CHOI GAP-BOK CONTORTED HIMSELF ENOUGH TO SQUEEZE THROUGH A MINUSCULE OPENING.

WHEN:	WHERE:	WHO:	CONVICTION:	OUTCOME:
SEPTEMBER 17, 2012	DAEGU CITY POLICE DEPARTMENT, SOUTH KOREA	KOREAN CHOI GAP-BOK, A ROBBER AND MASTER YOGI	ARRESTED ON SUSPICION OF ROBBERY	HE WAS CAUGHT A FEW DAYS LATER AND SENT BACK TO PRISON

THE PRISONER
CHOI GAP-BOK

Choi Gap-bok, age 49, was arrested on suspicion of robbery on September 12, 2012. The police took him to Daegu Metropolitan Police Station (in South Korea), where he was kept in a detention cell while awaiting trial.

This was, however, not the suspect's first detention—Gap-bok was a professional robber and had been in and out of jail several times, having spent a total of 23 years in prison.

AN OUTSTANDING YOGA MASTER

CHOI GAP-BOK, WHILE PRACTICING YOGA DURING ONE OF HIS PRISON TERMS.

DURING HIS MANY YEARS IN JAIL, CHOI GAP-BOK DEVOTED HIMSELF TO PRACTICING YOGA, AND HE BECAME A HIGHLY QUALIFIED MASTER IN THIS FIELD.

AN OUTSTANDING PLAN

THE PRISONER QUICKLY REALIZED THAT HE COULD USE HIS YOGA SKILLS TO ESCAPE FROM HIS PRISON CELL

NOT EVEN ONE WEEK

Apart from being a con man, Choi Gap-bok was also a resourceful character. On this particular occasion, he spent less than five days in detention.

The yogi came up with an escape idea that was as simple as it was surprising. He would squeeze himself through a small opening in the door intended for food deliveries. It was an uncomplicated but ingenious idea. Nobody imagined that a person could escape through such a tight slot.

OIL AND LITTLE ELSE

The plan required little preparation. Gap-bok studied the guards' routines and the doors leading out of jail. He also obtained an oily body lotion that would help him slip out.

THE ESCAPE IN STEPS

1. OIL & PILLOWS

At around 5 a. m., before dawn but after completing his yoga exercises, Choi Gap-bok oiled his skin all over with the body lotion to make slipping under his cell's bars somewhat easier. He was ready to give it a try.

To make sure the prison guards didn't suspect anything and didn't notice his absence, the yogi placed pillows under his blanket to make it look as if he was asleep.

2. THE GAP

He then lay on his back on the ground and tried to squeeze through the food slot faceup, but he was unsuccessful.

For his second attempt, he laid facedown and turned his head to the side, which allowed him to slide it through.

He then pushed under first one arm, then the other. His rear end got stuck, but he solved the problem by taking his pants off!

HE SLIPPED OUT THROUGH A GAP 18 INCHES WIDE AND 6 INCHES HIGH

3. PRISON OFFICERS

CHOI GAP-BOK COMPLETED HIS FEAT IN LESS THAN ONE MINUTE, MOVING WITH THE AGILITY OF AN OCTOPUS

Once outside his cell, he put his pants back on and snuck past the three guards at their work desks.

Finally he jumped out onto the street through a window.

4. ESCAPE TO THE MOUNTAINS

From Daegu Police Station, Choi Gap-bok ran to a nearby house, where he stole a car as well as a credit card.

HE DROVE SEVERAL MILES DOWN THE ROAD UNTIL HE SPOTTED A POLICE ROADBLOCK AHEAD

Choi had to abandon the car 200 yards from the checkpoint. He proceeded on foot and went to hide in the mountains.

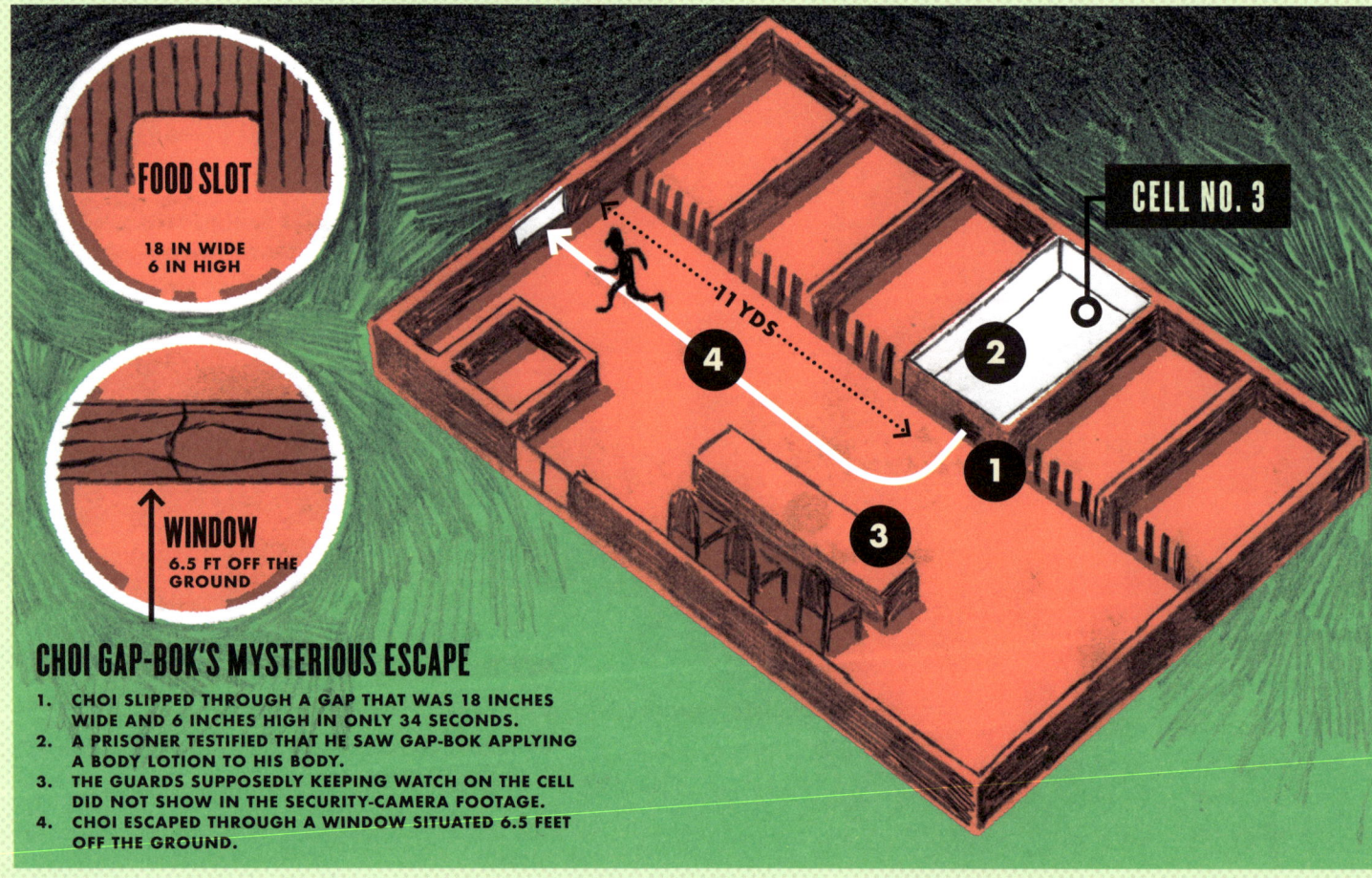

FOOD SLOT
18 IN WIDE
6 IN HIGH

WINDOW
6.5 FT OFF THE GROUND

CELL NO. 3

11 YDS

CHOI GAP-BOK'S MYSTERIOUS ESCAPE

1. CHOI SLIPPED THROUGH A GAP THAT WAS 18 INCHES WIDE AND 6 INCHES HIGH IN ONLY 34 SECONDS.
2. A PRISONER TESTIFIED THAT HE SAW GAP-BOK APPLYING A BODY LOTION TO HIS BODY.
3. THE GUARDS SUPPOSEDLY KEEPING WATCH ON THE CELL DID NOT SHOW IN THE SECURITY-CAMERA FOOTAGE.
4. CHOI ESCAPED THROUGH A WINDOW SITUATED 6.5 FEET OFF THE GROUND.

THE YOGI MANAGED TO FLEE THE CITY AND SEEK REFUGE ON NAMSAN, A NEARBY MOUNTAIN WHOSE KOREAN NAME MEANS "MOUNTAIN OF THE SOUTH."

POLICE MANHUNT

IT WAS NOT UNTIL AFTER 6 A. M. THAT THE GUARDS REALIZED HIS ABSENCE. IN TOTAL, 70 MINUTES HAD PASSED SINCE HIS ESCAPE.

A SECURITY LAPSE

The guards confessed that they had fallen asleep for part of the night. They also admitted that they had been distracted by browsing the Internet.

THE GUARDS' NEGLIGENCE WAS KEY TO CHOI'S SUCCESSFUL ESCAPE

The South Korean police started a large-scale manhunt lasting several days. They set up highway checkpoints and used helicopters and tracker dogs.

The crafty robber hid in the mountains. He managed to remain unnoticed as he only moved about at night.

HE MADE A MOCKERY OF THE POLICE FORCE FOR NEARLY ONE WEEK

Approximately 400 policemen were mobilized in Miryang, a city located 19 miles south of the escape site, when they were informed that several people thought they had seen Gap-bok.

ZEROING IN ON THE SUSPECT

After six days of intense searching, Gap-bok was finally discovered on the rooftop of a building in Miryang and detained. The fugitive insisted that he was innocent but was sent straight back to the police station from which he had escaped.

This time around, the slot through which food was delivered to his cell was only 4 inches high and 5 inches wide.

NOW IT WAS UNLIKELY THAT THE YOGI WOULD SLIP OUT AGAIN

LaJornada

SATURDAY, JULY 11, 2015

MEXICO, FEDERAL DISTRICT · YEAR 31 · NUMBER 11.027 · www.jornada.unam.mx

10 PESOS

ESCAPE OF

THE WORLD'S MOST FAMOUS DRUG LORD ESCAPES FROM MEXICO'S EL ALTIPLANO MAXIMUM-SECURITY PRISON

"EL CHAPO"

HIS GANG BUILT A MILE-LONG TUNNEL EQUIPPED WITH VENTILATION, LIGHTS, AND TRACKS.

THE AUTHORITIES MADE SURE THERE WAS NO WAY OF ESCAPING THE HIGH-SECURITY PRISON WHERE "EL CHAPO" WAS INCARCERATED.

JOAQUÍN "EL CHAPO" GUZMÁN
THE WORLD'S MOST WANTED MAN

THE US OFFERED A REWARD OF $5 MILLION FOR THE CAPTURE OF "EL CHAPO," WHO HAD BECOME THE WORLD'S MOST WANTED MAN FOLLOWING THE DEATH OF OSAMA BIN LADEN.

Joaquín Guzmán Loera, known as El Chapo ("Shorty") for his short stature, was born in a small rural village in northern Mexico.

He worked with local drug traffickers from a young age and learned everything he could from them. When the leader of the Mexican drug-trafficking ring was imprisoned, the 35-year-old El Chapo set up the Sinaloa Cartel and took his place.

El Chapo built a network of tunnels connecting Mexico with the United States and sent vast quantities of drugs to Mexico's northern neighbor.

Within barely four years, the Sinaloa Cartel grew to become one of the world's most dangerous criminal organizations.

RECOMPENSA
DE HASTA:
$5,000,000 DE DÓLARES
POR INFORMACIÓN QUE CONTRIBUYA A SU ARRESTO

Joaquín Guzmán Loera "El Chapo"

Everything was going along well when in 1993, El Chapo was caught by police near Chiapas, on the border between Guatemala and Mexico.

THE AMERICAN AUTHORITIES OFFERED A $5-MILLION REWARD FOR THE CAPTURE OF CHAPO.

PRISON
PUENTE GRANDE

The head honcho of global drug trafficking was first held prisoner at Federal Social Rehabilitation Center No. 1 for two years. With a 20-year sentence hanging over his head, he was then transferred to the maximum-security Puente Grande prison.

El Chapo continued to lead the cartel from his luxurious cell, enjoying all manner of privileges by way of bribes and coercion.

AT PUENTE GRANDE, HE WAS KNOWN AS "EL JEFE" (THE BOSS)

ESCAPE FROM PUENTE GRANDE

But El Jefe served only nine years of his sentence at the Puente Grande jail. He escaped on January 18, 2001, hidden in a laundry cart.

He had bribed 15 officers to turn a blind eye at the six security checkpoints on the way to the exit.

EL CHAPO'S ESCAPE FURTHER CEMENTED HIS ICONIC STATUS

He spent 13 years living as a fugitive, moving around the sophisticated system of tunnels connecting his regular haunts. It was very difficult for the police to determine his whereabouts. The intelligence agencies in both the United States and Mexico cooperated for several months to recapture him. Theirs was a top-secret operation involving a "mole," or informer.

Finally, on February 22, 2014, El Chapo was caught in the tourist town of Mazatlán on the Pacific.

THE OPERATION WAS A SUCCESS—NO SHOTS FIRED, NOBODY INJURED

A heavy security detail transferred El Chapo to the El Altiplano maximum-security prison. Located approximately 56 miles west of Mexico City, it was considered the most secure prison in Latin America. No inmate had ever managed to escape its walls.

TO PREVENT ANY RESCUE ATTEMPT BY HIS GANG, NO INFORMATION WAS GIVEN AS TO WHERE OR WHEN HE WAS BEING TRANSFERRED

PLANNING THE ESCAPE

CONTACT WITH THE OUTSIDE WORLD

Prisoner El Chapo also received "special" treatment at the El Altiplano jail. He continued to run his criminal operations from prison and, of course, also planned his escape from there.

THE HOUSE

The escape plan involved digging a huge tunnel, which had become his primary means of escape.

His children bought a residence near the prison and set to work on getting it dug right away.

A GPS WATCH

The tunnel engineers managed to obtain the exact coordinates of El Chapo's detention cell using a GPS-enabled watch.

BRIBES

Neighbors who complained about the drilling noise were silenced with bribes.

THE TUNNEL

The engineers spent nearly a year drilling and excavating a sophisticated, mile-long tunnel featuring lighting, ventilation, and tracks.

EVERY DAY WAS A DAY CLOSER TO THE ESCAPE

THE ESCAPE IN STEPS

El Chapo planned his escape for Saturday, June 11, 2015. It was a known fact that the prison had reduced security surveillance on weekends.

1. THE SHOWER

El Chapo was in his prison cell (No. 20) watching television, just like any other Saturday evening. At 8:52 p. m., after a few fierce hammer blows, he heard a voice through the shower drain announcing that everything was ready.

El Chapo calmly put on his shoes, lifted the shower trapdoor and slipped through a hole that his accomplices had dug for his escape.

The shower was entirely hidden from view by a wall, creating a blind spot in the cell, which the security cameras were unable to monitor.

2. ACCESSING THE TUNNEL

All El Chapo had to do now was go down the stairs his accomplices had put in place to descend the 33-ft-long shaft that linked up with the tunnel.

3. THE TUNNEL

The tunnel ran for a good mile underneath the El Altiplano prison. It was fitted with lights, ventilation, and a motorcycle converted to run on rail tracks—El Chapo's accomplices had used the bike to remove the dirt they had excavated.

A COLLABORATOR TRANSPORTED THE FUGITIVE TO THE EXIT ON A MOTORCYCLE

EL CHAPO SQUATS DOWN AND DISAPPEARS DOWN A HOLE THAT REMAINED OUT OF VIEW OF THE SECURITY CAMERAS.

"EL CHAPO" GUZMÁN ESCAPED FROM THE MAXIMUM-SECURITY PRISON WHERE HE HAD BEEN HELD SINCE FEBRUARY 2014

8:52 P.M.

Guzmán went to the shower. When the cameras hadn't picked him up for a while, the guards were sent to his cell. They found it empty.

EQUIPMENT FOUND

1. VENTILATION PIPE
2. OXYGEN TANK
3. LIGHTING SYSTEM
4. TOOLS, FUEL, AND VARIOUS FORMS OF BUILDING MATERIALS

THE ESCAPE ROUTE

1 Underneath the shower in his cell was a space measuring 20×20 inches and 1.5 feet deep.

20 in

EL ALTIPLANO

A MAXIMUM-SECURITY FEDERAL PRISON

HALL 2 CELL NO. 20
EL CHAPO'S CELL IN THE SPECIAL-TREATMENT AREA

2 This led to a 33-foot vertical shaft and a ladder.

33 feet

5 The exit was located in a field not far from the prison.

3 This ladder in turn led to a tunnel that was more than a mile long.

4 A motorcycle adapted to operate on tracks served as a means of transportation.

1 mile

LaJornada

4. SANTA JUANITA

The tunnel ended at a house under construction, which his children had purchased for the operation.

5. BY HIGHWAY AND LIGHT AIRPLANE

From the house, El Chapo traveled by quad bike to a secret warehouse where he was met by the van that would transport him to the city of San Juan.

WAITING FOR HIM IN SAN JUAN WAS HIS PILOT "CACHIMBA," WHO WOULD FLY HIM TO SINALOA, HIS PLACE OF RESIDENCE

THE HOUSE WAS LOCATED NORTHWEST OF THE PRISON, IN THE SMALL VILLAGE OF SANTA JUANITA.

A CLANDESTINE TRACK WAS USED AS A RUNWAY FOR THE PLANE THAT TOOK EL CHAPO TO HIS SAFE HOUSE.

INVESTIGATION

EL ALTIPLANO ON ALERT

It took 25 minutes for the security guards who operated and watched the CCTV cameras to notice that there was no prisoner in cell No. 20.

When the two guards entered the cell, they spotted the 20-inch circular space that had been opened under the shower drain. However, it took at least another 20 minutes before anyone came to check on what was going on.

The length of time it took for the security guards to respond would remain one of the great mysteries of the escape.

EL CHAPO'S ESCAPE HIGHLIGHTED THE EXISTENCE OF CORRUPTION AT MEXICO'S TOP-SECURITY PRISON

POLICE MANHUNT

The prison reported the escape, and law-enforcement agencies issued a red alert.

EL CHAPO HAD ESCAPED AGAIN AND WAS MAKING A MOCKERY OF THE MEXICAN LAW-ENFORCEMENT AGENCIES

THE NEAREST INTERNATIONAL AIRPORT WAS CLOSED AND HIGHWAY CHECKS SET UP IN SURROUNDING STATES

The police entered the tunnel and followed it to the house. All they found were tools, oxygen tanks, fuel cylinders, piping, and other objects that the engineers had used to build the escape route and then abandoned. Not a trace of El Chapo.

ACCOMPLICES

Although the prison was built like a fortress, it had also succumbed to El Chapo's corrupt forces.

All prison staff at the El Altiplano jail were detained right away and questioned by police.

18 OFFICERS FROM EL ALTIPLANO WERE SUSPECTED OF COLLABORATING WITH THE DRUG LORD

THE FILM
Mexican movie *Chapo. El escape del siglo* (2016) (*Chapo. Escape of the Century*) recounts Guzmán's jailbreak.

THE UNITED STATES

Six months later, El Chapo was recaptured in the city of Los Mochis (state of Sinaloa), but this time he was extradited to the United States, where he was tried in what was considered to be the trial of the century.

THE JURY HANDED EL CHAPO A LIFE SENTENCE FOR DRUG TRAFFICKING AT THE MOST HELLISH PRISON IN THE US. HE REMAINS INCARCERATED TO THIS DAY (FOR THE MOMENT...)

THE NAVY LED AN OPERATION WITH OTHER FEDERAL AGENCIES THAT RESULTED IN THE RE-CAPTURE OF THE SINALOA CARTEL'S HEAD HONCHO.

WANTED:

HENRY BROWN

HENRY BROWN MANAGED TO ENDURE AN ARDUOUS 27-HOUR JOURNEY HIDDEN IN A MAILED BOX. **HE ACHIEVED FREEDOM FOR LIFE.**

GIACOMO CASANOVA

THE VENETIAN ESCAPED THE DREADFUL DUNGEON OF "THE LEADS" PRISON. **HE HAD BEEN CHARGED WITH BLASPHEMY.**

JOHN H. DILLINGER

A POPULAR ROBBER, HE WAS SO GREATLY FEARED THAT HE COULD ESCAPE FROM PRISON WITH A HOMEMADE WOODEN GUN.

MANY AMERICANS CONSIDERED HIM A HERO WHO WAS FIGHTING AGAINST THE SYSTEM.

ALFRED "HOUDINI" HINDS

NO HIGH-SECURITY PRISON WAS TOO MUCH FOR HIM. ALFRED HINDS WAS A HIGHLY INTELLIGENT MAN AND HE EVENTUALLY BECAME AN EXPERT IN LEGAL MATTERS.

FRANK MORRIS
& THE ANGLIN BROTHERS

WE DON'T KNOW IF THEY SURVIVED THEIR DANGEROUS RAFT JOURNEY FROM ALCATRAZ TO THE MAINLAND, OR IF THEY DIED IN THE PACIFIC.

DISAPPEARED ONE NIGHT FROM THEIR CELLS AT ALCATRAZ.

CHOP GAP-BOK

THE KOREAN ROBBER DEFIED THE POLICE AT DAEGO CITY POLICE STATION WITH HIS UNBELIEVABLE ESCAPE.

HE ACHIEVED THE IMPOSSIBLE.

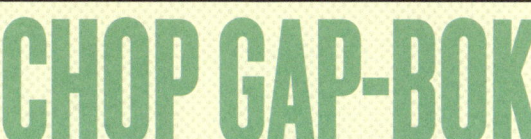

38
WOMEN

THEY FLED THROUGH MONTEVIDEO'S SEWER SYSTEM WITH THE HELP OF FELLOW MEMBERS OF THE TUPAMAROS GUERRILLA GROUP.

THEY ALL MANAGED TO ESCAPE.

TWO
FAMILIES

THE EIGHT ESCAPEES FLED EAST GERMANY, CROSSING THE BORDER BETWEEN THE TWO HALVES OF THE COUNTRY, AND LIVED IN WEST GERMANY THEREAFTER.
THEIR DARING FEAT MADE THEM POPULAR MEDIA PERSONALITIES.

JOAQUÍN
"EL CHAPO"
GUZMÁN

THE DANGEROUS MEXICAN CRIMINAL VANISHED FROM THE EL ALTIPLANO PRISON DESPITE THE SECURITY CAMERAS FITTED IN HIS CELL.
HIS BUDDIES RESCUED HIM VIA A MILE-LONG TUNNEL.